Revise for GCSE
Geography NEAB B

John Smith

Heinemann Educational Publishers
Halley Court, Jordan Hill, Oxford OX2 8EJ
A division of Reed Educational and Professional Publishing Ltd

Heinemann is a registered trade mark of
Reed Educational & Professional Publishing Ltd

OXFORD   MELBOURNE   AUCKLAND
JOHANNESBURG   BLANTYRE   GABORONE
IBADAN   PORTSMOUTH NH (USA)   CHICAGO

First published 1998

01 00 99 98
10 9 8 7 6 5 4 3 2 1

British Library Cataloguing in Publication Data
A catalogue record for this book is available from the British Library

ISBN 0 435 10139 0

Typeset and designed by Magnet Harlequin, Oxford
Printed and bound in Great Britain by the Bath Press, Bath

Contents

How to use this book

One of the great advantages of studying Geography is that it is all about real places and real processes. We can see geography going on in the world around us all the time. When we study geography we can go out into the field, or we can look at photographs, videos, satellite images, etc. and actually see what we are studying. We can marvel at wonderful and strange places – but we can also find much that is interesting about more familiar, local, everyday places.

Geographers therefore try to see **patterns** in what they observe. All cities have certain things in common; all climates are linked together by the circulation of the winds; all rivers erode, transport and deposit material; and so on. Geographers have developed a series of key concepts or key ideas or theories to describe these patterns. When they know the key ideas well they can predict many things about new places, because they fit patterns that have already been studied. There are also special features about places, which make each one different from all other places. We have to study the patterns, but also the special features that make places unique and give them their 'sense of place'.

NEAB Syllabus B

Many GCSE syllabuses provide teachers and students with a set of key ideas, then leave them to choose which areas they study to illustrate those ideas. Syllabus B starts off by choosing areas that **must** be studied, and then picks out key ideas which can be seen clearly in those chosen regions. There are three scales of study:

- The United Kingdom (UK)
- The European Union (EU)
- The Wider World.

In the syllabus content for the UK, some areas of study have been specified clearly. For example, everyone has to study:

- farming in East Anglia and the Lake District
- ports on the east coast
- high-tech industry in the M4 corridor

and so on. Each of the specified regions is thought to be the best place to study a particular key idea.

However, with some other topics teachers and students are left free to choose exactly which areas they study. The reason for this is that it would be rather unfair for a school in Birmingham to have to study urban growth and change in Manchester, for instance, when the key ideas could be illustrated just as well in their own city.

When people move on to study the EU and the Wider World the areas of study are specified very clearly. In the EU you must study:

- farming in southern Italy
- the Ruhr industrial region
- tourism in Mediterranean Spain
- the Rhine waterway
- the growth of Rotterdam/Europort.

Three of these topics are closely linked, and could be combined in one study.

In the Wider World you must study Amazonia, the Ganges Delta and Japan.

You must remember, though, whether you (or your teacher) have chosen certain places to study, or whether the syllabus has told you particular areas that you must study. You will be expected to have detailed knowledge of real places to gain high-level marks in the exam. Facts must be learnt!

Each paper in the exam has a quite separate content. Learn the UK topics for Paper 1 and the EU and the Wider World topics for Paper 2.

The structure of the assessment

There are three parts to the assessment for NEAB Syllabus B.

Paper 1 consists of questions on the UK. Both the Foundation and Higher tier papers are 1½ hours long. They consist of four structured questions, and all of them must be answered. At least one question will be based on an Ordnance Survey map at a scale of 1:25 000 or 1:50 000. This paper is worth 33 per cent of the final mark.

Paper 2 consists of questions on the EU and the Wider World topics. There is also a question that considers how the topics and regions studied relate to the whole world. (This is referred to as 'the global dimension'. You will not be expected to learn specific details about the rest of the world for this question, but you will be expected to show an understanding of how geographical ideas can be applied to the whole world.) There are five questions on both the Foundation and the Higher papers. Each lasts for 2 hours and is worth 40 per cent of the final mark.

The questions on both Paper 1 and Paper 2 are structured. Some sections need short answers, or even ticking of boxes or underlining words. Other questions have to be answered in extended writing. Detailed knowledge of case studies is required on both papers.

Coursework consists of a single geographical enquiry. It is worth 25 per cent of the final mark. It is not tiered.

How does this book use case studies?

Case studies form a very important part of all geography courses. They are studies of real places. They illustrate the key ideas that also form part of the course. For example, when you are studying glaciated landscapes, you look at:

- general ideas about how ice erodes
- general ideas about the formation of physical features like corries, arêtes and U-shaped valleys
- examples of these features and the way they fit together to form a landscape – for example, you could study the Helvellyn region of the Lake District as a case study to show how the processes have formed a real place.

In your exam you will be asked to 'refer to examples you have studied' or to 'illustrate your answer with references to case studies'. When you answer these questions you **must** write about real places. The examiner will check to see whether you write with a **sense of place**. In other words, you need to show that you know why a particular place is special, or different from other places. You need to know names and details of features

in the area that you are describing. If you include plenty of precise detail, the answer becomes a good one and your mark gets better.

Some revision books give detailed case studies for the whole Geography GCSE course. This book gives detailed studies for areas that are specified in the syllabus, especially places in the EU and the Wider World. However, some parts of the syllabus, mostly in the UK section, do not specify which places should be studied. Key ideas are given which can be illustrated by any case study, and any good example can be used.

You have spent two years studying a set of case studies. If this book gave you a completely new set you could waste a lot of time. Learning new case studies at this stage of the course could mean a lot of extra work, and maybe create a lot of confusion too. So this book tries to help you to *use the examples from your class work in the most efficient way possible.*

When you have to refer to one of your own case studies there is a box in the text headed 'Case Study questions'. This suggests what is essential to learn from any relevant place you have studied. At this point you could:

- write notes in your notebook (or in this book, if it is your own)
- write a summary of your case study in your notebook or clip it into this book
- write down page references in your notebook or in this book, to show which page of your exercise or textbook contains the information needed.

Marginal notes

Special notes are included on the right-hand side of many pages. These are simply some facts and ideas that could be used in your exam answers. Try to remember them, though they are not always key ideas.

Hints and Tips! These give general advice and useful information about how to prepare for and then sit the examination. Following this advice could stop you wasting time and effort *and* help you improve your grade.

These are useful facts and ideas that could provide helpful points in some of your exam answers.

 This is useful additional information about certain points in the text.

 One piece of advice for preparing for exams is: '**Active revision** (or doing things to help you remember) is usually better than **passive revision** (or just reading)'. The Focus Points give you little tasks to do to check that you are remembering what you have read.

Do the tasks set. Jot down your answers in your notebook, or ask a friend or parent to test you. Be honest with yourself.

- If you do well you should be pleased.

- If you do badly, do not despair. Just re-read the section, but more carefully this time. Then test yourself again and hope to do better.

- You have tested your 'short-term memory'. How long will the information stick? Next time you come to do some revision you may well test yourself again. Renewing your revision like this often helps transfer the information into your medium or long-term memory, which is very important for the exam.

- Many of the Focus Points ask you for four or five facts. Often two or three will be enough in the exam. So, why learn five?
  - It gives you something in reserve.
  - All the facts may not go into your long-term memory – but some will.
  - A full list of points helps you to *understand* as well as to learn.

Test questions

Each section ends with a test question, similar to the ones you may face in the exam. After each part of these questions there is a note like this: **(3 marks)**

This tells you how many marks the question is worth. It also provides a rough guide to the amount of detail needed in your answer.

- A 1 mark question usually requires a single word or short sentence.

- 2 mark questions may need two simple points, or they may need one point that has been elaborated or developed. Often the Hints and Tips (see above) explain how to develop and elaborate your answers.

- 3 mark questions almost certainly need some development of ideas – but usually only require three or four lines of writing. If you write much more you may be wasting time. If you write much less your answer may lack detail.

- When more marks are available the answer usually needs extended writing. Here are real chances to show your detailed knowledge and understanding. These longer answers usually need careful reference to your case studies.

Pages 126–135 give mark schemes, specimen answers and some advice on the best way to answer the questions.

Finally . . .

Good luck. Work hard, but . . .

- Try to enjoy your revision. It should be very satisfying to see the whole subject come together at the end of the course. You become a real geographer in this way, and real geographers impress examiners!

- Don't panic. Methodical, careful, steady work is far better than desperate over-cramming.

- Fit, relaxed, alert people do better in exams than burnt-out swotaholics.

- In the last few weeks before the exam, practise topics that you are not so good at. Do not just concentrate on what you are comfortable with. Work hard on your areas of weakness.

The United Kingdom

1 Urban growth and change

For this topic you should study:
- the traditional industrial town – its growth and morphology (or layout)
- the influence of coal and steam on urban growth and distribution and density of population
- urban structure and the development of conurbations
- causes and effects of inner city decline
- urban renewal, modern housing estates, commuter villages and changes to the urban fringe
- population movement, i.e. rural to urban and urban to rural migration, the drift from North to South, and journeys to work.

The growth, characteristics and morphology of industrial towns

Towns first developed as places where farmers came together to trade their surplus produce. Other functions then developed but large-scale industry was not attracted to towns until the Industrial Revolution. Then the growth of factories changed many towns completely.

The main changes that caused the Industrial Revolution were:

- the development of steam power

- the invention of machines that could use steam power in mines, e.g. for pumping water out or lifting minerals to the surface

- for transport, especially trains

- in factories, e.g. spinning and weaving cloth, shaping metal.

These new inventions led to great changes in the way of life of people throughout Britain. They led to:

- rapid growth of coal mining

- the development of railways to move coal and other raw materials

- the use of coal to power factories

- the movement of people to the factories to provide their workforce.

This caused enormous changes in the functions and shapes of towns in Britain, especially on the coalfields of northern England, Central Scotland and South Wales. During the nineteenth and early twentieth centuries, factories became concentrated in industrial areas close to town centres. This was because they needed to be:

The great period of railway building in Britain was 1840–60. Sites close to the railways were the main location for industry until after the First World War.

- close to sources of raw materials and fuel, especially coal, which was very bulky and difficult to transport

- close to canals, railways or ports, where bulky raw materials arrived

- close to the crowded areas of workers' housing, which was built as close as possible to most town and city centres.

Industrial towns

Some industrial towns were built on coalfields, but many more got their supplies of coal by rail or boat. In these towns industry grew around the railway, canal or port. The coal could be brought in fairly cheaply by rail or water, but it was very difficult and expensive to move it far from the terminals. Most towns specialized in one or two main types of industry. Most needed large quantities of raw materials, and these too were brought in by rail or water. Examples of the industries which developed include the following:

- Tyneside and Wearside   iron and steel, shipbuilding
- Teesside   iron and steel, chemicals
- West Yorkshire   woollen textiles, engineering
- South Yorkshire   iron and steel, engineering
- Lancashire   cotton textiles, engineering
- Merseyside   shipbuilding, food processing, chemicals
- Staffordshire   pottery
- West Midlands   metal working
- East Midlands   textiles
- South Wales   iron and steel
- Swindon   engineering
- Gravesend   chemicals

Focus **Point 1**

Cover the page. List three factors that led to the concentration of industry around town centres in the nineteenth and early twentieth centuries.

Hints and Tips!

You will not be expected to know all of these examples, but you need to learn two or three of them. Try to mark those you learn on a map of the British Isles.

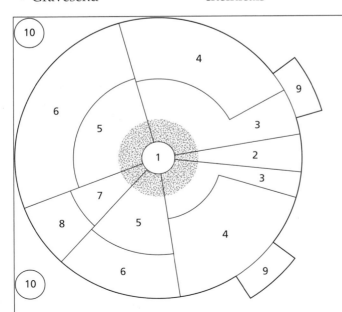

1 = CBD
2 = Heavy industry along river/railway/canal
3 = C19 and early C20 workers' housing
4 = Mid and late C20 council housing
5 = C19 and early C20 mid quality housing
6 = Mid and late C20 mid quality housing
7 = C19 and early C20 high quality housing
8 = Mid and late C20 high quality housing
9 = Out of town industrial estates
10 = Commuter villages
= Redevelopment areas

◀ *A model of urban structures in UK towns*

Although there were many different types of industry, the layout (or morphology) of all these industrial towns followed a very similar pattern, or model.

Questions

> Choose an industrial town which you have studied.
> 1 Draw a sketch map to show how it grew in the nineteenth and early twentieth centuries.
> 2 Mark on your map some or all of the features shown on the model. The model shows where these features might be, in theory. You should show where they were actually found in your town.
> 3 Add names of parts of the town, individual factories, roads, etc. where possible.

The development of conurbations

As the industrial towns were growing in the nineteenth and early twentieth centuries, there were few planning regulations to control their spread. Individual settlements developed in a random way as entrepreneurs built factories and houses in the places that were cheapest and most convenient. A number of factors caused towns to spread.

- Industry spread along the banks of rivers, and along railway lines.

- As road transport developed, towns spread along main roads, in a process called **ribbon development**.

Focus Point 2

Think of an area in your case study town which illustrates each of the ideas in this list.

Hints and Tips!

Learn this definition: 'A conurbation is found where several towns and/or cities have spread until they merge and form a single, large urban area.'

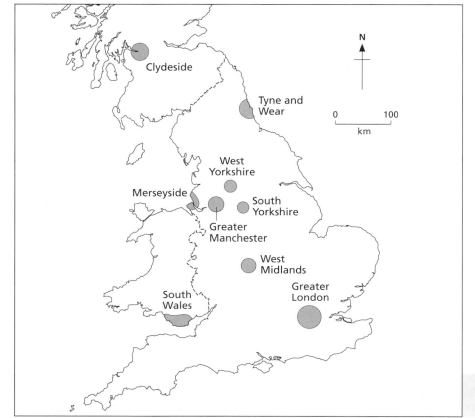

◄ *Conurbations in Great Britain*

- It is cheaper to build on new sites than to clear old buildings away and reclaim used land. The development of **greenfield sites** on the edges of towns caused the built-up areas to spread.

All these processes helped to cause the development of **conurbations**. This term was first used in 1915 to describe South Lancashire. Towns and cities including Manchester, Salford, Oldham, Bury, Rochdale, Bolton and others had all spread outwards and started to merge, especially along the main roads, railways and canals. They did not form a continuous built-up area. There were still patches of park, farmland, woodland, etc. around all these towns, but the urban sprawl around the edges of towns was threatening the few remaining open areas.

Other conurbations developed in Central Scotland, Tyne and Wear, West Yorkshire, Merseyside, the Potteries, West Midlands, South Wales, Greater London and along the south coast. Some geographers even suggest that a 'super-conurbation' is developing which stretches from Preston in the north-west to Dover in the south-east!

Since 1945 planning regulations have tried to limit the spread of conurbations in the UK. Local planning controls and Green Belts have been imposed to try to conserve areas of open countryside around the edges of the main built-up areas. Since the mid-1980s a lot of funding has been put into inner city areas to try to attract development back there, and to reduce the pressure on the urban fringes.

Some geographers would go even further. They talk about **Europolis**, a conurbation which stretches from the English conurbations across the Channel to include Rotterdam and other built-up areas in the Netherlands, the Ruhr conurbation in Germany, parts of Belgium, and northern and eastern France! Look for this area in an atlas.

Questions

Draw a sketch map of a conurbation that you have studied. Mark and name:
- the main towns and cities
- places where built-up areas have merged
- areas of open space in between the spreading settlements
- the Green Belt, if it exists in that conurbation.

Inner city decline

The inner city areas of the industrial towns were built to suit nineteenth-century conditions. By the middle of the twentieth century they had become serious problem areas. The problems included the following.

- Slum housing – this was often poorly built and very crowded.

- Lack of open space – housing was crowded with no room for private gardens or public open space in inner city housing areas.

- Air pollution – coal-powered factories, houses heated with coal and fumes from transport all pollute the air, causing lung diseases.

- Traffic congestion – the volume of vehicles increased on roads built before the days of mass car ownership and lorry transport.

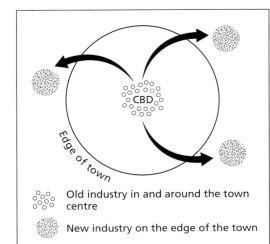

CBD

Edge of town

Old industry in and around the town centre

New industry on the edge of the town

▲ *Movement of industry out of towns*

The movement of industry from the inner cities
After about 1930 transport by lorry started to become very important for some industries, especially the new, light industries. The owners of the new factories wanted to avoid the crowded, old industrial areas. Many new factories were built along main roads leading out of the town centres. The new buildings were usually lighter and more spacious than the old factories. They were built fairly close to the new suburban housing that was spreading outwards at this time.

As road transport became more and more important, new factories were built further from the centres. Many were built on industrial estates at the edges of towns and cities.

Advantages of industrial estates	Disadvantages of inner city industrial sites
• Easy access to motorways, ring roads and by-passes.	• Congested, with narrow roads built for smaller lorries and less road traffic.
• A clean, attractive environment, close to open countryside and fresh air.	• Old buildings in a noisy and often polluted environment.
• Land is usually cheap.	• Land is more expensive because of restricted area.
• 'Greenfield sites' do not need expensive work to make them fit for new building.	• Old 'brownfield' sites often need expensive demolition and reclamation before new building can take place.

Questions

1 For your case study town or city, name and describe:
   • a nineteenth-century industrial area
   • a mid-twentieth-century industrial area on a main road
   • a late-twentieth-century industrial estate, built on a by-pass.

2 For each example that you have named, give three reasons why it developed in that particular place.

Focus Point 3

Cover up this table. Give three reasons why industry has moved from inner city areas to industrial estates on the edges of built-up areas.

Housing change in inner cities
Many people have moved out from inner cities since 1930. At the same time there has been much redevelopment of inner city housing.

1 **Slum clearance** – many large areas of old terraced housing which had become unfit for human habitation have been knocked down. Much of this old housing was built in the nineteenth century and lacked basic amenities like inside toilets, hot and cold running water and damp-proofing.

2 **High-rise housing** was built to replace the slum housing. Many residential tower blocks were built between about 1950 and 1975. This was a fairly cheap way to provide housing with all modern facilities. Unfortunately the flats were often badly built and suffered from condensation, expensive heating systems, vandalism, broken lifts, isolation of people in the flats, etc. They were often unpopular, and many of these flats have either been demolished or redesigned without the higher floors.

Pushes from inner cities	Pulls to suburbs
• Housing was old and run-down.	• New, better-designed housing.
• Land was expensive, so houses were small.	• Land was cheaper, so houses could be larger.
• Little space for gardens or car parking.	• Plenty of space for gardens and car parking.
• Roads congested.	• New roads, designed for mass car ownership.
• Noisy and polluted by industry and traffic.	• Cleaner, greener environment.
• Social problems increased: crime, drugs, prostitution, etc.	• Fewer, less obvious social problems.
• Increasing unemployment as industry left.	• Increased employment as industry moved in.
• Shops and services left the inner city as people moved out and out-of-town shopping increased.	• Many new services and shopping centres built in suburbs and out-of-town locations.

3 **Low-rise/high-density housing** was built later. Such housing had to be quite compact, because the land was expensive, but it was designed to give people privacy. The estates were designed with large areas of public open space. These areas caused many problems because no one had responsibility for them.

4 **Housing regeneration** By the 1980s the worst slums had been cleared from most towns and cities. It became possible to improve the old housing without knocking it down. It is cheaper to keep old houses and add kitchens, bathrooms, fire escapes, new roofs, damp-proof courses, etc. Such work does not destroy communities. It causes less social disruption than the old slum clearance and redevelopment.

> **Note** At the end of the First World War, many politicians talked about knocking down the slums and building new houses for the soldiers coming home from the trenches. These would be 'Homes fit for heroes'. Unfortunately many of the old slums were not demolished until the 1960s.

Patterns of housing in towns and cities

Geography students need to understand where different types of housing are found. Housing often changes as one moves away from the city centre towards the edge. In general terms the pattern is like this:

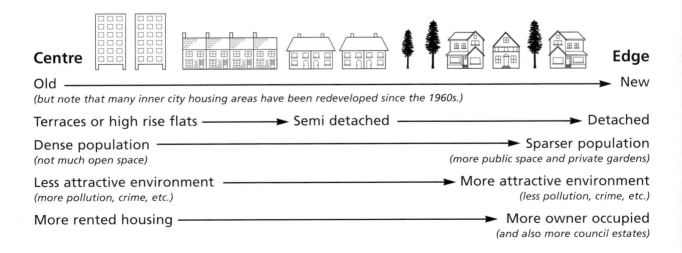

Centre ——————————————————— **Edge**

Old ————————————————————→ New
(but note that many inner city housing areas have been redeveloped since the 1960s.)

Terraces or high rise flats ——→ Semi detached ————————→ Detached

Dense population ———————————————→ Sparser population
(not much open space)   *(more public space and private gardens)*

Less attractive environment ———————————→ More attractive environment
(more pollution, crime, etc.)   *(less pollution, crime, etc.)*

More rented housing ————————————————→ More owner occupied
                                               (and also more council estates)

Questions

1 For your case study town or city, describe the types of housing found in named examples of:
   - inner city areas
   - inner suburbs
   - outer suburbs
   - rural–urban fringe.

2 Some people say 'The quality of housing in towns improves as you move from the centre to the edges'. Is this hypothesis true in your case study town?

3 Some cities are described as having **concentric rings** of housing types. Others have **sectors**. Does your case study fit either of these models?

Population movement in the industrial towns

(a) Decline in inner city population

The figures below show how Manchester's population has changed. They are typical of what happened in many towns and cities in the UK.

Manchester's population

Year	Total population
1931	766 311
1951	703 082
1961	662 021
1971	543 859
1981	462 500
1991	438 500
1996	430 818

There were two main reasons for the changes.

1 The fall in the average size of households was partly due to falling birth rates. It was also partly due to young people leaving home earlier to start their own families and to set up their own homes.

2 The decline in the number of houses in the city centre was due to slum clearance. Between 1951 and 1980, 83 255 houses were demolished in Manchester, and only 59 468 new ones were built in the city (23 344 houses were built by the council on overspill estates outside the city boundaries).

(b) Changes to the rural–urban fringe

Middlesbrough is a town that has been losing population too, but these figures show how the number of households has risen, and is predicted to go on rising.

Middlesbrough's population

Year	1981	1991	2001(est.)	2006(est.)
Population	150 000	144 000	143 000	140 000
Households	54 000	55 600	57 800	58 300

DID YOU KNOW ?

◆There has been a census in Britain once every 10 years from 1801 to the present, except in 1941 when the country was at war.

◆Note that the population of Manchester fell by almost 120 000 (about 18%) in just 10 years after 1961. This was the peak period for slum clearance in the inner city.

People want more houses. They do not want to live in inner city areas. Therefore a lot of new houses have had to be built on 'greenfield sites' on the edges of urban areas. The two maps show how the built-up area of Middlesbrough has expanded southwards, into the countryside. This has formed the new suburb of Coulby Newham. Most of the land that was built on used to be farmland, although it was not very high quality.

There has also been growth of commuter settlements in areas outside the old towns. Some commuter settlements are in rural villages which have expanded as new estates have been built. Other commuter settlements are in completely new towns.

(c) The move from north to south
The map below shows population change in the UK. It shows:

- decline or only slow growth in most of northern England, Scotland, Wales and Northern Ireland

- fast decline in the major conurbations, including London

- rapid growth in south-east England (outside London), the south-west and East Anglia

- growth in rural areas close to conurbations.

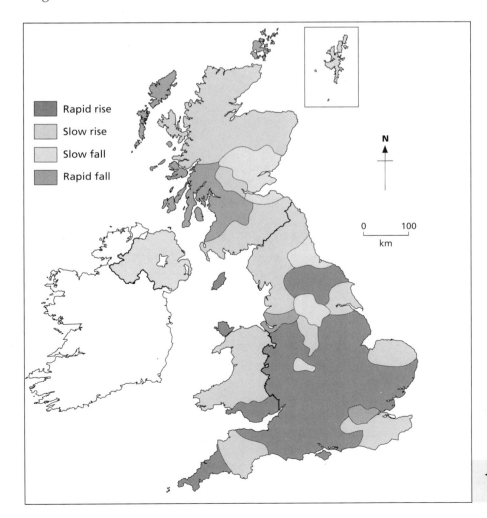

ocus Points 4 and 5

◆ Give two **push factors** that made people want to leave inner city areas. Give two **pull factors** that attracted them to suburban housing areas.

◆ In 1981 the average number of people in households in Middlesbrough was:
$$\frac{150\ 000}{54\ 000} = 2.8 \text{ people.}$$
In 2006 it is estimated that the average household size will be
$$\frac{140\ 000}{58\ 300} = ? \text{ people.}$$

◀ *Population change in the UK, 1961–91*

Exam practice

(a) Name an industrial town or city in the UK that you have studied.

   (i) Name an industry which was found in that town in the nineteenth century.   (1 mark)

   (ii) Give one reason why your chosen town was well suited for that industry
      to develop.   (2 marks)

   (iii)Where did housing develop for the people who worked in your chosen industry? (2 marks)

   (iv)Describe the appearance of the houses in that area, and describe the
      area's street pattern.   (4 marks)

(b) Many old areas of workers' housing have been redeveloped since the 1960s.
    Name an area of redevelopment in your chosen town or city and:

   (i) explain why the area needed to be redeveloped   (4 marks)

   (ii) describe how the redevelopment has altered the area.   (4 marks)

(c) With reference to one or more examples you have studied, explain why commuter villages
    have grown up around the edges of many towns and cities in the UK.   (3 marks)

2 The farm as a system

For this topic you should study:
- inputs, processes and outputs of a commercial farm
- the influences of the natural and economic environment on farming systems in the UK.

You should make particular studies of:
- hill sheep farming in the Lake District, with reference to
  - physical constraints of landform, climate and soil, including a study of relief rainfall
  - a farm case study
  - the effect of diversification
- arable farming in East Anglia, with reference to
  - the physical advantages of landform, climate and soil
  - a farm case study
  - changing effects of economic conditions on farming (demands of consumers, supermarket chains, food canners and freezers, etc.)
  - technology and environmental issues (hedgerow removal, wetland drainage, etc.)
  - conservation and its effects on farming
  - diversification and set-aside.

Classification of farms

The natural environment – soil, climate, slope and relief – has a big effect on what can be grown on any farm. It allows some crops to be grown, but makes it impossible to grow certain others. For instance, in East Anglia wheat, grass, barley, rye, oats and sugar beet will all grow, but rice and bananas will not, because the temperature is too low. In other words, the farmer can choose what to grow, within limits.

The human environment also affects the farmer's decisions. What he chooses depends on his knowledge, skills and interests and also on the prices he can get for each crop at the market. He is also influenced by government policies which may make some crops more attractive by paying subsidies, and may make others less attractive by putting quotas (or limits) on the amount that can be grown.

It is very useful for geographers to be able to classify farms into different groups. It makes studying farming easier if we identify the key features of different farming systems. All farms – in the UK and in other parts of the world – can be classified in three ways. These put farms in groups depending on their inputs, processes and outputs.

Note Some geographers think that human influences on farmers are more important than physical influences these days. Farmers can change the physical environment using technology – but they cannot change the needs of the market. The policies of the European Union also have an enormous effect on what farmers produce.

Hints and Tips!

You should try to learn the three classifications that follow.

First learn the shapes of the tables and the headings in each box. This gives you a structure, so later it is much easier to learn the detail under each heading.

Classification by inputs

INTENSIVE FARMING	EXTENSIVE FARMING
These farms have large amounts of inputs on a comparatively small area of land. They are usually found on good land. Money and time invested in such land will bring good profits for the farmer. **Capital intensive** Invests a lot of money in machinery, seeds, fertilizers, irrigation, etc. **Labour intensive** Puts a lot of work into a small area of land. **Capital and labour intensive** Invests a lot of money, and uses a lot of labour.	These farms have comparatively small inputs for large areas of land. They are usually found where conditions are poor, so it is not worth farmers putting a lot of money or work into the land.

Classification by processes

Arable Grows crops, mainly cereals such as wheat, barley, maize and sugar beet.	**Pastoral** Keeps animals for meat, milk, wool, etc.
Mixed Usually combines arable farming with keeping some animals.	**Market gardening** Grows fruit, flowers or vegetables.

Note Mixed farming used to be **very** common in most parts of England. In the last 40 years farming has gradually become more specialized, often because of pressure from the government or the EU. This means that mixed farms are now less common here.

Classification by outputs

Commercial The outputs from the farm are mainly or entirely for sale.	**Subsistence** The outputs of the farm are eaten or used by the family who run the farm. In good years there may be some produce left over for sale.
Mainly subsistence The family rely on food produced on the farm, but always plan to try and produce some surplus for sale.	

Farm systems

ocus Point 1

Cover the page then write simple definitions of:

- arable
- pastoral
- subsistence
- commercial
- labour intensive
- capital intensive
- extensive.

Questions

A system diagram for any farm shows its inputs, processes and outputs. From your studies of farms in the Lake District and East Anglia you ought to be able to complete the charts on the next page by filling in the boxes. Use a key word or phrase in each space to summarize the important features of the farm.

Lake District _Beckside Farm_ (name of farm or area)

Physical inputs	Human inputs	
Climate	**Labour**	**Capital**
Temperature _Cold most of the year_	Only employs one regular farm worker to help him, but he makes good use of 5 sheep and neighbouring farmers lend him a hand	Machinery _tractor, 2 trailers a grass cutter, hay baler and muck-spreader_
Rainfall[1] _Wet_		Seeds/stock _rape, oats, barley and Kale_
Sunshine _not much_		Fertilizer _~_
Land		Pesticides _—_
Soil _Rocky_		Irrigation _Natural irrigation_
Relief _Steep_		Other _—_

The farm — Area of land _40l hectares_
Buildings _200 year old farm house_

Main processes _Sheep farming_   _Crops grown_

Outputs[2]
lambs to _Penrith_   _barley_ to _Penrite_
ewes to _Penrite_   _Kale_ to _fed to cattle_

1 See the section on 'Relief rainfall' below.
2 This could include other sources of income. See the section on 'Diversification' below.

East Anglia _Croghan farm_ (name of farm or area)

Physical inputs	Human inputs	
Climate	**Labour**	**Capital**
Temperature _Warm in MJJAS_	3 full time men. Farmer hires firm to spray crops with insecticide	Machinery _Plough - Seed drill - tractor - Combine harvester and baler_
Rainfall _Through out the year_		Seeds/stock _wheat suger beet and barley_
Sunshine _In AMJJAS_		Fertilizer[3] _Pig and poultry_
Land		Pesticides _Incesticide_
Soil _Medium light loam_		Irrigation _Some_
Relief _light slope_		Other

The farm — Area of land _104 hectares_
Buildings _Chicken houses_

Main processes _Crop varied._

Outputs[4]
straw to _sold to pet shops_ _Barley_ to _animal feed_
wheat to _sold to miller_ _Sugar beet_ to _British Sugar corporation factory_

3 See the section on 'Intensive farming and the environment' below.
4 See the section on 'Diversification' below.

Relief rainfall and farming in the UK

One of the main differences between the environments of the Lake District and East Anglia is in terms of their rainfall.

	Rainfall in the Lake District	Rainfall in East Anglia
Total	At least 1000 mm/year. Over 2000 mm/year in places.	Below 750 mm/year everywhere. Below 600 mm/year in places.
Distribution	All year round but autumn/winter maximum.	All year round but late summer maximum.
Cause	Relief and frontal rainfall.	Frontal, with convective rainfall in summer.

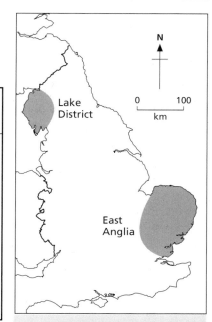

▲ The Lake District and East Anglia

The diagram below shows why the Lake District receives so much rainfall, and why rainfall totals are much lower in East Anglia.

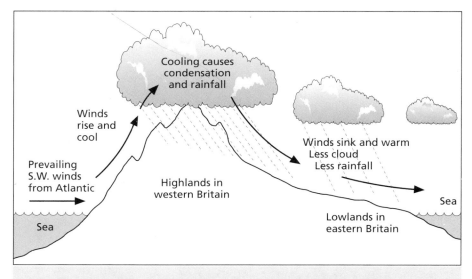

▲ Causes of heavy rainfall in the west and rain shadow in the east

Hints and Tips!

Learn this diagram carefully and precisely. Clear use of statistics like these can gain you extra marks in the exam.

Focus Point 2

Cover up the diagram and then draw your own labelled diagram to explain:
- how relief rainfall is formed
- what a rain shadow is.

Intensive farming and the environment

Until the 1970s almost all farms in the UK were mixed farms. They grew some crops and kept some animals. This had a number of advantages:

• Animals provided manure to help fertilize the soil.

• Crops were fed to animals, and meat made more profit than cereals.

- The workload was spread out through the year.

- If the weather was bad for one product, something else did well.

- Different crops used different minerals from the soil. Rotation kept the soil fertile.

However, from the 1970s arable farmers began to specialize in just one or two crops. This was mainly because **subsidies** were paid by the EU. It was also a result of the need to buy specialized machinery, and to develop specialized skills in the workforce. Mechanization and the development of **monoculture** (production of a single crop) did cause problems, but farmers came up with solutions to these. Unfortunately the solutions often caused new problems.

Problem	Solution	New problems
No animals on farms = no manure, so less fertile soil.	Increase the input of chemical fertilizers.	Overuse of chemicals pollutes soil, rivers and drinking water.
Monoculture = less crop rotation so nutrients not replaced.	Increase the input of chemical fertilizers.	Loss of wildlife, because of chemicals and loss of habitat.
Monoculture = large areas with one crop so disease spreads easily.	Increase the input of pesticides.	
Mechanization = more space needed for machines to work efficiently.	Pull up hedgerows to make fewer, larger fields. Drain wetlands.	Soil erosion. Loss of beauty in the landscape.
Overproduction = too much crop grown so price falls.	EU guarantees prices and stores surpluses.	High cost to taxpayers.

Diversification of farming

In the last few decades farmers intensified production; now they are being encouraged to cut production in some areas. **Diversification** means that farmers are encouraged to look for new ways of using the land. In some areas of the country farmers can receive subsidies for some or all of the following developments:

- farming land by less intensive, traditional methods to encourage wild flowers to grow in grassland

- replanting hedgerows, and trimming them in such a way that they provide good habitats for a variety of wild animals and birds

- planting woodland instead of crops

- leaving some areas as wildlife reserves, rather than growing crops

- leaving wetland in its natural state and not draining it, and so on.

Even when there is no new land use, farmers can leave land unused and receive a payment in compensation. This is called **set-aside**, and up to 10 per cent of a farmer's land can be left, or 'set aside'. The aim is to cut overproduction and surpluses kept in storage by the EU. It also gives land

Hints and Tips!

When you know the general ideas shown on this table, you need to learn extra details about the problems by referring to your case study notes. The relevant section in your notes might be headed: 'Intensive farming', 'Drainage of wetlands' or 'Hedgerow removal'.

a chance to lie fallow (rest), and improve its fertility without adding more chemicals. While it is unused it becomes a better habitat for wildlife.

Farmers are also encouraged to diversify their income by using their land for other purposes. For example they may:

- convert old farm buildings as holiday homes
- offer bed and breakfast at the farm
- stock streams with fish and let fishermen pay for the right to fish
- keep unusual animals for meat, such as deer or even ostriches
- use some fields for sports meetings, such as motorbike scrambling

Soil erosion in East Anglia

It is easy to take soil for granted. People who do not work with soil often think of it as 'dirt'. In fact soil is wonderfully complex and delicate, and is essential for human life. Soil is made up of:

- minerals – fine particles of broken and weathered rock
- humus – a crumbly, black substance, formed from the decomposition of dead plant and animal material
- water – which is held in the soil by the humus
- air – which fills the pore spaces between the mineral particles
- organisms – like bacteria which break down waste to form humus, and larger creatures like worms, which mix the soil.

Healthy soil has a good 'structure'. Mineral particles and humus become bonded together, and hold moisture. This forms little 'crumbs' that are roughly the size and shape of breadcrumbs. A soil like this contains the nutrients needed for plant growth. The plants provide roots which help bind the soil together. They intercept some of the rainfall and protect the soil from water erosion, and they can break the force of the wind.

Poor farming can destroy soil structure. This happens when the farmer takes too much out of the land, without recycling humus back into the soil. The crumb structure is lost and the soil becomes loose and dusty, and can easily be washed away by water or blown away by wind. In East Anglia the effect of a combination of policies has been a serious increase in soil erosion, as shown in the table.

The erosion in East Anglia never became as serious as in some parts of the world, like the Sahel in Africa or the 'dust bowl' of the USA, but it was clear that the attempt to increase output from the land was damaging the soil. In the 1990s the Common Agricultural Policy (CAP) of the European Union (EU) has attempted to stop or even reverse the

Hints and Tips!

This is an ideal topic to show your understanding of how values and attitudes can affect the way different groups see the countryside.

◆ Dairy farmers used to produce hay as winter feed for cows. Grass was cut from late June onwards and dried in the sun. Now most farmers produce silage. Grass is cut earlier and then pickled to preserve it. Some farmers are paid a subsidy to make hay instead. It is cut later so the flowers produce seeds for the next year.

Hints and Tips!

You can remember the five components of soil by giving it the brand name WHAMO!

This stands for Water + Humus + Air + Minerals + Organisms.

Focus Point 3

Cover up the page then list:

◆ three ways that some farmers can get subsidies for farming to conserve the environment

◆ three ways that farmers can diversify into new ways of using the land.

• Increased use of fertilizers reduced use of manure.	• Less humus returned to soil, so crumb structure was damaged.
• Increased mechanization.	• Heavy machinery compressed soil, less infiltration of rain water, more run-off.
• Reduction of pastoral farming, grass ploughed up for crops.	• Ploughing leaves soil without vegetation cover, so no roots to protect soil.
• Removal of hedges.	• Nothing to break the force of the wind, so erosion is increased.

damage that was done to the soil. Now the CAP encourages farmers to reduce the intensity of their farming by:

- paying subsidies to farmers who replant hedgerows
- paying them to 'set aside' land, which allows the soil to recover, and also provides land for wildlife
- encouraging diversification.

Exam practice

(a) (i) The Lake District has heavy rainfall, over 1000mm per year in many places. Draw a labelled diagram to explain how the area's high land helps to cause the heavy rainfall. (? marks)

  (ii) Explain why East Anglia has average rainfall totals that are lower than those for the Lake District. (4 marks)

(b) Explain why the relief of East Anglia is well suited to arable farming, and why the relief of the Lake District is unsuited to arable farming. (5 marks)

(c) Diversification of land use has become common in many farming areas of the UK. Choose an example of diversification that you have studied in **either** the Lake District **or** East Anglia.

  (i) Describe how diversification of land use has happened.

  (ii) Explain the advantages to the farmer. (6 marks)

Hints and Tips!

The CAP is a complex subject, but if you can learn some of the basic ideas included here you could earn marks in the exam.

 ocus Point 4

◆ List four changes to farming in East Anglia that have helped to increase soil erosion.

◆ List four ways that farmers have been encouraged to reduce the problem of soil erosion.

3 Electricity generation

For this topic you should study:

- the location of power stations (gas, coal, oil and nuclear) and reasons for the locations
- advantages and disadvantages of each type of power station, including impact on the environment
- alternative power sources, e.g. wind, wave, solar.

If you refer back to Chapter 1 Urban growth and change, or look ahead to Chapter 5 Manufacturing industry, you will see that the development of electricity in the twentieth century has had an enormous effect on many aspects of our life. When electricity replaced coal as the major source of power in industry, it allowed factory location to become far more 'footloose'. Entrepreneurs were no longer tied to locations on the coalfields or close to ports and railways.

Electricity is a very easily transportable form of power. Yet when power stations which generate electricity are being built, great care has to be taken over their location. Most power stations are not at all footloose.

Location of thermal power stations

Coal-fired stations

- Must be near large supplies of coal because it is bulky and very expensive to transport.
- Need large amounts of cooling water.
- Must be large for economies of scale.
- Often linked to pits by special loop railways that only carry coal.
- Built along major rivers, especially the Trent and the Aire in the Notts/Yorks areas.
- Only built in ideal locations.

Coal is no longer economic, and causes serious pollution problems. No new building is likely, and old stations may be run down.

Oil-fired stations

- Must be close to oil supplies.
- Also need cooling water.
- Must be large for economies of scale.
- Built close to coastal oil refineries and linked by pipelines.
- Are near rivers or the sea.
- Only in ideal locations.

Oil is too expensive and scarce for power stations now. No new ones are being built.

Gas-fired stations

- Need access to gas – but it is the most easily transportable source of fuel.
- The most footloose of all thermal power sources.
- Should be close to a gas pipeline terminal.

Small and medium-sized stations are economic. The 'dash for gas' in the late 1980s/90s led to the building of several new stations. More may follow.

Hints and Tips!

You should know at least two factors that influence the location of each type of power station.

ocus Point 1

Cover up the pages. Describe the location of one example of each of the following types of power station:

- nuclear
- HEP
- coal-fired
- gas-fired.

Give the reasons for each of the locations you have described.

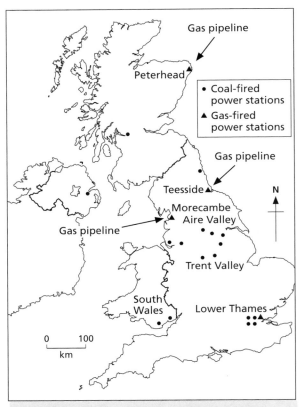

▲ *Some coal-fired power stations and recently-built gas-fired power stations*

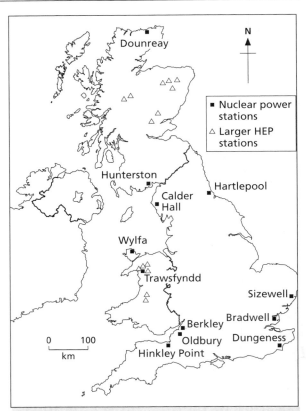

▲ *Some of Britain's nuclear power stations and larger HEP stations*

Nuclear power stations

- Need large areas of flat land, underlain by stable rocks.
- Need very large amounts of cooling water.

- Were originally built away from dense population, because of risk during development.
- The risk is no longer so great, but there is still much opposition.

- All on the coast, except Trawsfynnydd, which is on a lake.
- Were originally in isolated areas of the north and west, but later plants were nearer the cities.
- Any new plants will probably be built fairly close to the market, i.e. the conurbations.

The cost of development of new power stations is very great. So is the cost of closing old ones. It is unlikely that any new plants will be built in the next ten years at least.

HEP stations

- Need a large and reliable supply of water: heavy rainfall and low evaporation.
- Suitable sites for reservoirs: stable impermeable rock, cheap, sparsely populated land to flood.
- Need a large 'head' of water.
- Land of low landscape value preferred.

- Highlands in north and west.

- Few suitable large rivers in UK highlands.
- Rules out most areas in National Parks.

There are very few potential sites with streams big enough to make investment worthwhile. Little scope for further development.

Questions

Refer to examples of power stations that you have studied.
How do the factors described above fit your case studies?

Advantages and disadvantages of different forms of power stations

Renewable or non-renewable
- HEP is renewable.

- Nuclear power uses only very small amounts of raw materials, and it is possible to recycle and re-use spent nuclear fuel.

- All fossil fuels are non-renewable, but:

Coal – there are large supplies left but they are deep and therefore difficult, expensive and dangerous to mine.

Oil – it is estimated that the world's proven resources will last for another 25 years. However, oil is very valuable as a raw material and as fuel for transport, so it is wasteful to use it for generating electricity.

Gas – is often found with oil. Some is piped to houses but in the past much was burnt off as waste. There has been a recent rush to build gas-powered power stations. North Sea supplies may only last for about 20 years. Imports can replace it after that, but gas supplies will not last for ever.

Impact on the environment

Positive	Negative
HEP	
• Does not cause any air pollution.	• Dams in highland valleys cause visual pollution.
• It does not produce waste.	• Land is lost when valleys flood, but is usually of low agricultural value.
Nuclear	
• Does not produce CO_2, which contributes to global warming. • Does not produce sulphur nitrogen oxides, which contribute to acid rain.	• Nuclear waste is dangerous and difficult to dispose of safely. It can remain toxic for many decades. There is much fear of spills and accidents, although the safety record of the UK's nuclear industry is good. Safety costs are very high. This form of power is still being developed and long-term effects are not completely understood.
Coal	
• Coal power has been used for a long time, so it is well understood.	• Releases carbon dioxide which is the biggest cause of the greenhouse effect and global warming.

Hints and Tips!

Questions often ask about the advantages and disadvantages of the various types of power station. The issues are complicated. No one type of power has all the advantages. None has all the disadvantages. Try hard to write a fair and balanced answer.

Fitting 'scrubbers' to the chimneys of coal-fired power stations can remove almost all the sulphur which causes acid rain. However, if they were fitted to all the UK's coal-fired power stations it would add 10% to our electricity bills. Is it worth the cost?

Positive	Negative
Coal cont.	
• New technology means emissions of damaging gases can be reduced – but at a cost.	• Burning releases sulphur and nitrogen oxides, which are the main cause of acid rain. • Mining and transport of coal also causes environmental damage.
Oil	
• Oil-fired power stations are smaller than coal and nuclear stations, so there is less visual pollution.	• Like coal, oil contributes to the greenhouse effect and acid rain. • Production and transport of oil causes environmental damage.
Gas	
• Much cleaner and less polluting than coal or oil. • No problem of waste disposal like nuclear has.	• Produces some carbon dioxide, but far less than coal or oil.

Relative costs

It is very difficult to obtain figures for the relative costs of the different forms of power generation. Probably, in terms of cost per unit of energy, the five main sources can be put in this order:

Cheapest ⟶ Most expensive
Gas   Coal   HEP   Oil   Nuclear

Employment prospects

In any discussion of energy supplies, the size of the workforce has to be considered. Modern electricity generation is very capital intensive. Modern power stations cost enormous sums to build, but they are very mechanized so they only employ a small labour force. However ...

• Coal mining employed hundreds of thousands of men up to the 1960s. Now it employs fewer than 20 000. If any more coal-fired power stations are closed the mining industry will shrink still further.

• Nuclear power stations make a big contribution to employment in some areas. Sellafield in west Cumbria is the major employer in an area with few other sources of employment, except tourism.

• New gas-fired power stations need a very small workforce.

What can be done to reduce the threat of global warming?

Most world leaders now accept that global warming is a threat, and that something needs to be done about it. It seems certain that responsibility for action will lie mainly with the more economically developing countries (MEDCs). They have been, and still are, the main polluters. In addition, they can better afford to bring in the changes. There are two different types of response to the threat.

Hints and Tips!

In many coalfield areas the closure of the pits still makes people very angry. If you are angry about a topic it is quite acceptable to let your anger show in a geography answer – as long as you support your arguments with clear facts and figures.

Global warming results from the greenhouse effect, which is caused mainly by emissions of carbon dioxide. It may lead to rises in sea-level. Do not confuse it with the destruction of the ozone layer, which is mainly caused by CFC emissions.

1 Plan now to reduce the damaging effects of warming.

2 Try to slow down warming by controlling greenhouse gases.

1 *How can we plan to reduce the effects of warming?*

Even the most optimistic forecasts for the reduction of emissions accept that some warming will still happen. Therefore the problem must be managed. This means that, over the next 50 years or so:

- People must plan to control floods caused by rising sea-levels. The Thames Barrage is one example of this being done, but the problems of places like Bangladesh are on a far larger scale.

- People must plan for water supplies in areas where drought might be caused by climate change. Already the UK has suffered water shortages in several areas. Even wet countries like ours need to introduce very efficient national water grids, so that resources can be used efficiently.

- People should attempt to 'drought-proof' agriculture. The development of strains of plants which use less water is probably important. More important is to develop techniques of farming that use water less wastefully. Conservation of water, like conservation of energy, will become more and more important.

The management of resources should be based on planning for sustainable development in all parts of the world.

2 *How can warming be prevented or slowed down?*

- At the Earth Summit in 1992 it was agreed that countries should reduce emissions of greenhouse gases to 1990 levels by 2010. Many, but not all, countries agreed to this.

- The Kyoto conference in 1997 tried to persuade countries to go further than this, and to start cutting emissions now. Europe and Japan promised to do so. The USA said this would be impossible for them, as it would lead to far too many job losses.

- The main way to reduce emissions is to reduce the burning of coal and oil. To help this people can:
  - use more renewable energy (see 'Development of alternative power sources' below)
  - use more natural gas, which emits less carbon than coal does
  - conserve energy in the home and in industry
  - plan transport policies to reduce the use of cars and lorries.

Development of alternative power sources

At the moment some attempts are being made to develop alternative sources of energy. None of these is commercially viable on a large scale yet, but at some time during the twenty-first century it will become essential to use one or more of these alternatives to produce most of our energy.

As fossil fuels become more scarce, the price of energy will rise. This will mean that research and development of alternative sources will become more and more profitable. Now there are many ideas about

ocus Point 2

Cover up the page. List four ways that countries/people can reduce the use of coal and oil, and so help reduce global warming.

possible ways of producing energy and the increased price will make development of these sources profitable. Unless they are developed, the developed economies may collapse.

The following are possible sources of the alternative energy supplies:

Wind – Wind-powered turbines have been built in many areas of highland and coastal Britain. At present they can provide power for small, isolated communities. Some wind farms also sell energy to the National Grid, but they are not profitable unless they are subsidized. For large-scale wind power supplies it would be necessary to build thousands of turbines which would cover very large areas of land.

Tidal power – As tides come in the water rises. As the tide goes out the water falls. High water could be kept back by a dam, then allowed to rush out through a turbine, producing electricity. Such a scheme has been built at La Rance in Brittany. Similar schemes could be built in suitable areas in the UK, such as the Severn Estuary or Morecambe Bay. They would be very expensive and would cause great change in the environments behind the dams but they could produce a lot of energy.

Solar power – The sun provides an enormous amount of energy to Earth. If this could be harnessed it would meet most of our needs. Some houses have been fitted with solar panels to heat water. If this can be stored it can be an important source of energy on a small scale.

Most people are familiar with solar power on an even smaller scale: you may well have a calculator powered by a solar cell, which uses the sun's energy to produce electricity. Some cars have even been powered

◆ Wind power does not produce any polluting gases, but it can damage the environment. The windiest places are often on hilltops in beautiful areas, and wind turbines can ruin the scenery.

◆ In 1998 Heaton Manor Comprehensive School in Newcastle upon Tyne should become the first school in the country to be fitted with solar panels as part of a national scheme to try to develop the use of alternative energy in schools. If the panels are successful there, the idea will be copied in schools across the country.

◀ Sites of possible development of alternative power sources

by experimental solar cells. This seems to be a very important area of research. In future, technology could be developed to use solar cells to generate a large proportion of our energy needs.

Geothermal energy – This is seen at its simplest in Iceland and New Zealand where magma reservoirs close to the surface heat water naturally. This water comes to the surface in springs and can be used for heating greenhouses, central heating of blocks of flats and offices, and even to generate electricity. In future it might be possible to generate electricity on a much larger scale by pumping water down to much deeper layers of hot rock, and using it to power turbines. However, research and capital costs would be enormous.

An experimental scheme in Cornwall is trying to produce electricity by pumping water down to hot rocks beneath the surface to produce steam. The early results of this project are quite promising.

Questions

Choose one or two alternative energy proposals for the UK which you have studied. Describe each scheme referring to:
- the way the scheme would work
- where the scheme would be sited, and why that area is suitable
- the advantages and disadvantages of the scheme for the local area and the country as a whole.

Exam practice

(a) On a map of the UK, mark and name:
   (i)   an area where coal is important for the generation of electricity
   (ii) an area where HEP generation is important
   (iii) a nuclear power station
   (iv) an area that may well be useful for generating electricity from an alternative energy source.   (4 marks)

(b) Give two reasons why the area you marked for (i) above is suitable for coal-fired power stations.   (4 marks)

(c) Give two reasons why the area you marked for (ii) above is suitable for HEP generation.   (4 marks)

(d) Nuclear power stations were originally built in remote parts of the country, but later ones have been built near to areas of dense population. Explain why.   (4 marks)

(e) Why is the government encouraging research into the development of alternative power resources, such as wind, wave and tidal power?   (4 marks)

4 River systems in the hydrological cycle

For this topic you should study:
- the hydrological cycle
- landforms and processes in uplands (V-shaped valleys, interlocking spurs, waterfalls) and lowlands (flood plains, braiding, meanders, ox-bow lakes, levées)
- watershed, drainage basin, catchment area
- water supplies in rivers, lakes and reservoirs, and groundwater supplies
- water supplies and rainfall distribution
- water management – flood control, pollution control, leisure and environment.

The hydrological cycle (or water cycle) shows how water is transferred from the sea to the land, then back again to the sea. Diagrams showing the cycle are very simplified. They often show all the water that falls onto the land flowing back to the sea, over the surface, as run-off. The full picture is more complicated, as a study of drainage basins shows.

Still, it is important to understand the basic features of the hydrological cycle. These show energy from the sun evaporating water. This evaporation can happen over land as well as over the sea.

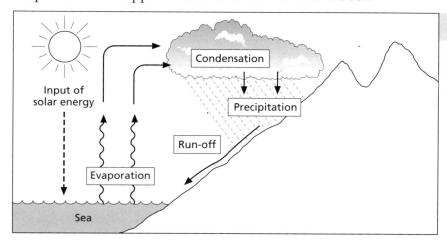

 *The hydrological cycle*

Focus **Point 1**

Cover the page and draw a labelled diagram showing evaporation, condensation, precipitation and run-off in the water cycle.

Learn this precisely.

Water vapour is then carried over the land, by winds. Here the air may be cooled, causing condensation, followed by precipitation.

The movement of water through a drainage basin

Water is input into the drainage basin by **precipitation**. This can take the form of rain, snow, sleet, hail, dew or frost. Then the water can pass through several types of **transfer**, or be kept in several different **stores**.

Transfers	Stores
Unchannelled surface flow	Snowfields or ice caps
Channelled flow in rivers	Lakes, ponds, puddles, etc.
Soil throughflow	Soil moisture storage
Groundwater flow	Groundwater storage (in permeable rocks)
Take-up by plants	
Evaporation*/Evapo-transpiration*	Storage as plant moisture

* These two transfers take water out of the river system.

Note: The transfers and stores listed are all natural processes. People can store water in reservoirs, tanks, etc. They can even pump water into the rocks to top up groundwater supplies for future use. Then they can transfer water along pipes, canals, etc. They can also pump water into rivers so that water supplies are transferred through these cheap, natural systems.

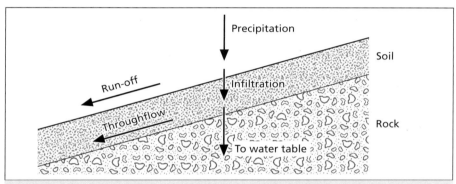

▲ *What happens to precipitation when it reaches the surface?*

Exactly which route water takes through the river system depends on many interrelated factors. These include:

Intensity of the rainfall – during light rain much of the water soaks into the ground. When rain is heavier it cannot all infiltrate. Run-off increases.

Length of rainfall period – if there has been a long period of rainfall the ground may be saturated. If there is any more rain it will lead to surface run-off.

Nature of the rock – if the rock is permeable (e.g. limestone) water can soak into it, and be stored as groundwater. Impermeable rock (such as shale) will not let water soak in, and this also increases run-off.

Vegetation cover – plant leaves intercept rainfall. This can slow it down, meaning it does not run off as quickly. Plant roots help to break up the soil, and allow water to infiltrate more easily, also reducing run-off.

Building and farming – when the surface is built over, with houses or tarmac, water cannot infiltrate. This increases the rate of run-off. Overgrazing by animals can compact the soil, and make infiltration difficult. The weight of heavy machinery on the land can also do this.

In fact, anything that reduces infiltration, or reduces the amount of water stored in the soil, or increases the rate of run-off, helps cause flooding. This is because these all lead to more water reaching the river quickly. When it all arrives at the same time, floods may result.

All rain is caused when air rises and cools, leading to condensation. The air can be forced to rise in three different ways: by convection, by relief, or at a front.

ocus Point 2

Cover the page, then list parts of the hydrological cycle: three natural transfers, three natural stores, two human transfers, and two human stores.

Remember: the faster rainwater gets to the stream, the more likely it is to cause a flood.

What is a drainage basin?

A river is a channel of running water. It is fed by water that runs into it, from a wide area. Some water reaches the main river through smaller rivers or **tributaries**. These join the main stream at **confluences**.

Any water that falls onto the surface in between the river and its tributaries runs towards one of the streams. It may flow over the surface (as **run-off**) or through the soil (as **throughflow**). At the bottom of slopes there is usually a stream, flowing in a **valley**.

The whole area drained by a main river and its tributaries is called a **drainage basin**. A basin is usually surrounded by higher land – except at the coast, where the river joins the sea. The highest land, which separates one river basin from the next, is called the **watershed**.

The map on page 100 shows the drainage basin of the Ganges river. To the north are the Himalayas and to the south is the Deccan Plateau. The river flows into the Bay of Bengal, through its **delta**. Here the river splits up into a number of smaller channels, called **distributaries**.

Landforms in drainage basins

As water moves through the drainage basin it has energy. Some of the energy is used to do 'work' of **erosion** and **transportation** of rock and soil. If the amount of energy available to the river is reduced it cannot do so much work, so some of the material that was being transported is **deposited**.

The amount of energy available is greatest when:	The amount of energy decreases when:
• the river is flowing steeply downhill	• the river's course becomes gentler
• the river contains a large volume of water.	• the volume of water in the river decreases.

Rivers erode by:

- **Hydraulic action** where the power of the moving water simply forces particles of rock away from the bed.

- **Abrasion** when the river knocks and rubs the material it is carrying against the bed, and this breaks more particles off the bed.

- **Attrition** where particles of rock being transported are rubbed together, and against the bed, and are worn away by the friction.

- **Solution** where rock is dissolved as the river flows over it.

Four forms of transportation can also be seen. They are shown on the diagram below.

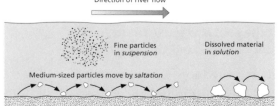

Movement of particles transported by a river

ocus Point 3

Would these actions make a flood more likely or less likely?
(a) Cutting down an area of woodland and ploughing the soil.
(b) Putting drains into an area of marshland, so that it can be used for arable crops.
(c) Reducing the size of a flock of sheep, to stop them over-grazing the land.
(d) Building a new housing estate on a hillside in a drainage basin.

ocus Point 4

Cover the page, then list the four ways that a river erodes, and the four ways that a river transports material.

Landforms in the upper sections

In the upland sections most of a river's spare energy is used to erode its bed. The bed is lowered more quickly than material can be removed from the sides. This produces a steep, V-shaped valley cross-section. As the river gets closer to sea-level the rate of downcutting gets slower and the sides are eroded more quickly. This means that the valley broadens out to form more gently sloping sides.

Hints and Tips!

Learn the headings (here, for erosion) first. Once you have learnt them it gives you a structure to fit the details into. This makes the details easier to learn.

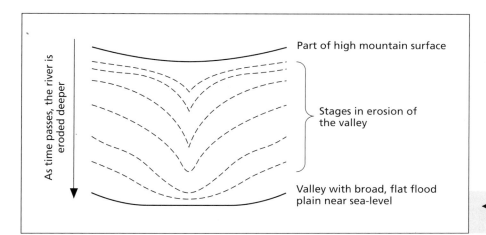

As time passes, the river is eroded deeper

Part of high mountain surface

Stages in erosion of the valley

Valley with broad, flat flood plain near sea-level

◀ *Stages in the erosion of a river valley*

Rivers never flow straight for a long distance. They always bend or meander. This produces the interlocking spurs that are found in river valleys in highland areas. As the rivers cuts its valley deeper into the rock the bends are cut into the surface. This leaves the area of land on the inside of each bend as a ridge of high land. The river twists and turns between these ridges, which are known as **interlocking spurs**.

Some people think that interlocking spurs look like the teeth of a giant-sized zip.

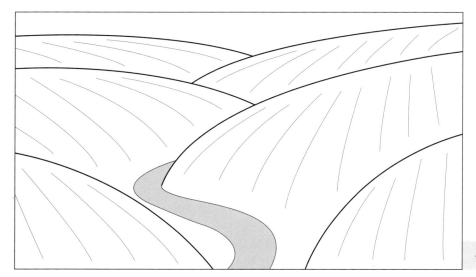

◀ *Interlocking spurs*

Sometimes a river bed is formed of a layer of hard rock which cannot easily be eroded. When the river passes from the hard rock onto softer

Learn diagrams

rock it is suddenly able to erode its bed easily, and so there is a sudden fall in the bed. This produces a **waterfall**.

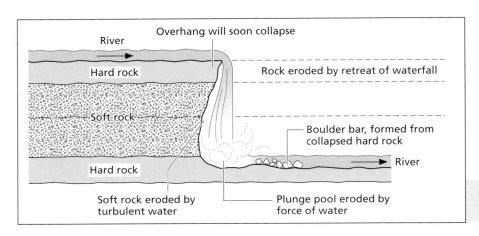

◀ *Formation of a waterfall*

Often a deep, steep-sided gorge forms downstream from a waterfall. This is because the water going over the falls has a sudden increase of energy. This can be used to undercut the hard rock at the top of the waterfall. The waterfall gradually retreats up the stream, leaving the gorge between the remains of the layer of hard rock.

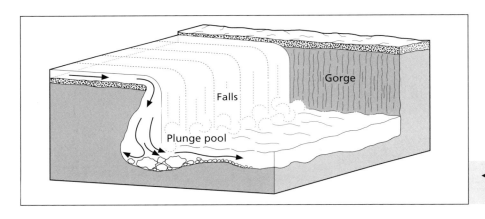

◀ *A gorge below a waterfall*

Landforms in the lower section

The diagram 'Stages in erosion of a river valley' on the previous page shows how V-shaped upland streams broaden out as they approach sea-level. Near the sea rivers flow in wide, flat valleys which cannot be eroded downwards, because they are so near sea-level. The rivers are broad and deep, so there is little friction with the sides. The rivers have plenty of energy, so they can transport a lot of sediment.

However, when a river floods it spreads out over a wider area. There is far more friction with the wider bed. Less energy is available for transportation, so a lot of sediment is suddenly dropped by the river. The whole flood plain can be covered with a thin layer of fine sediment. If this is repeated many times, a deep layer of rich soil can be built up on the flood plain.

Deposition of flood plains can be seen in parts of the UK but it is even more obvious in river valleys like the Ganges and Brahmaputra in India and Bangladesh. See Chapter 15.

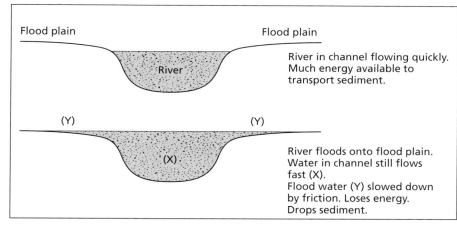

◀ *Flood plain formation*

When a river floods, sediment is not spread evenly. The moment that the water leaves the main channel it slows down. At this point it suddenly loses energy and so it deposits the material that it is carrying. This forms a narrow bank alongside the river. Repeated flooding can build up this bank to form a **levée**. Natural levées may offer protection from flooding, but, unfortunately, when the river returns to normal flow, it can deposit more sediment on its bed. This raises the bed, making it liable to flood again. If the bed and the levées are both raised, the flood risk can become even greater, as the river eventually flows above the level of the flood plain.

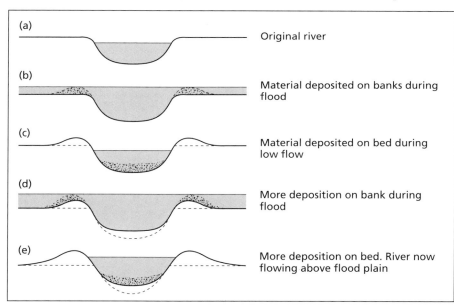

◀ *Levée formation*

DID YOU KNOW?

Flooding is a very serious problem in parts of the Rhine flood plain in the Netherlands. In 1995 very heavy floods threatened to burst the levées and flood large areas of densely populated land.

As rivers flow across their flood plains they meander. The main current swings from side to side as it flows, and this leads to erosion being concentrated first on one bank then on the other. Deposition always takes place on the opposite bank. Meanders form, and then grow. This can lead to the formation of ox-bow lakes.

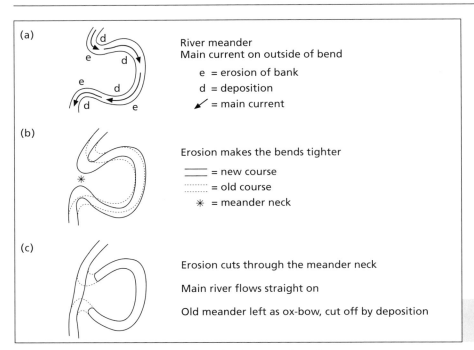

Hints and Tips!
You need to
know examples of
all the above
features located
in the UK.

◀ *Meanders and ox-bow lake formation*

Management of water in drainage basins

Water supply
The two maps below show that some of the heaviest rainfall totals in
the UK are in areas with sparse population. Some of the areas of dense
population have only moderate rainfall.

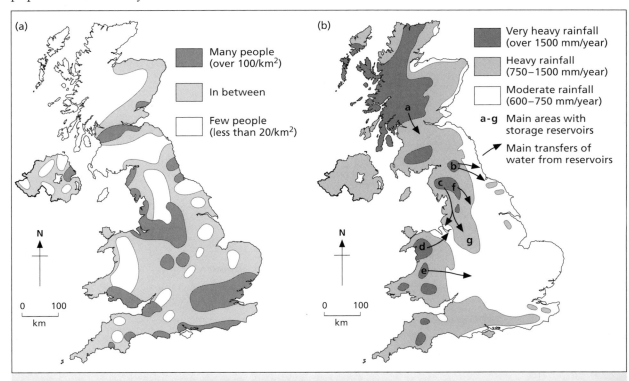

▲ *Population density, rainfall and water supply in the UK*
(a) Population density   (b) Rainfall and water supply

One of the main aims of water management is to store water which falls in places and at times when it is not needed; and to transfer it to the places where it is needed. These maps show how reservoirs are used for storage in wet, sparsely populated highlands. Then the water is transferred to the drier, densely populated lowland areas for industry, agriculture and domestic use.

Questions

1   Choose an example of a reservoir in highland Britain.
    • Why was the reservoir built there?
    • What area does it serve?

2   Think about any of the issues involved in the construction of the reservoir and its system of water transfer.
    Can the reservoir be used for other purposes, such as leisure?

In other areas water is obtained from boreholes, from rivers, or by treating and recycling waste water. The diagram below shows how these three sources of water are used to supply Greater London.

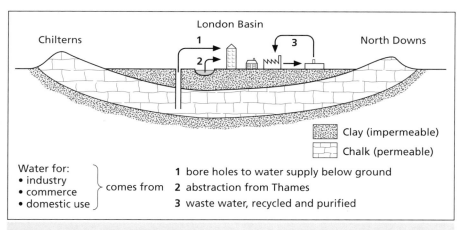

▲ *Greater London's water sources*

Flood control

Water authorities are responsible for trying to reduce the flood hazard caused by rivers. Some of the causes of floods are described at the beginning of this chapter. Ways of controlling floodwater include:

Reafforestation schemes – to increase evapotranspiration, reduce run-off and to hold the soil together.

Advising on land use – to try to reduce over-stocking and other farming practices that increase flood risk.

Clearing and straightening streams – to remove obstructions and speed flow of water through the system.

Zoning land use on flood plains – There are strict regulations to stop building in areas with a serious flood risk, and to allow only non-residential building in areas with some flood risk.

ocus Point 5

Study the two maps on page 36 along with a relief map of Britain in an atlas. Learn the names of the highland regions where precipitation totals are highest.

◆ Kielder Water in Northumberland is the largest artificial reservoir in Europe. One of the reasons it was built was to provide water for industry on Teesside. Soon after construction was started, this industry went into recession and the water has never been needed there in the amount that was expected.

◆ In many river valleys sports fields are built on flood plains. They are sometimes used to store flood water. This might mean someone misses their game of football. However, if it also mean that someone's house does not get flooded with filthy water, it is probably worth missing the football match!

Controlling river pollution

The water authorities and the Environment Agency share responsibility for controlling river pollution. In 1990 over 60 per cent of rivers in England and Wales were described as being of 'good quality', with another 25 per cent described as 'fair quality'. However, 11 per cent were 'poor' or 'bad'. In 1991 there were almost 30 000 reported pollution incidents. These came from:

The authorities first trace the source of the pollution then get it stopped. They try to prevent further incidents by talking to polluters. They may take them to court if negotiation and persuasion fail.

Managing water for leisure

The leisure industry is the fastest-growing area of employment in the world. It is very important in the UK. Many people spend a large part of their leisure on or next to water, boating, fishing, swimming, canoeing, bird watching, surfboarding, and doing many more such pastimes.

Many rivers and reservoirs are used for **multipurpose schemes**. Water that is being stored for water supply or HEP is also used for leisure pursuits. This multiple use of water needs very careful management.

- Is the water that is needed for leisure clean and healthy?

- Can the authorities be sure that leisure use does not pollute drinking water?

- Can conflict between the different users be reduced or stopped?

- Should leisure users be asked to pay for using the water?

Focus Point 6

Cover the page.

List three ways in which planting forests helps to reduce flooding.

List three other ways in which people plan to reduce the problems caused by flooding in river basins.

Untreated sewage	28%
Oil spills and leaks	24%
Farm spills and leaks*	13%
Industrial waste	12%
Other sources†	23%

* As well as reported incidents there is regular infiltration of chemicals from fertilizers etc. spread on the land.

† Including pollution from roads, power stations, landfill sites, leisure activities, etc.

Questions

Refer to a reservoir or river that has multiple uses.

1   Describe the varied uses.

2   Explain how potential conflicts between users are managed and resolved.

Exam practice

(a)   Choose **one** of the features of a river valley listed below:

- waterfall and gorge   • ox-bow lake   • levées.

(i) Name a place where an example of this feature can be found.   (1 mark)
(ii) Describe the appearance of your named feature.   (3 marks)
(iii)Using one or more diagrams, explain how the feature was formed.   (5 marks)

(b)   (i)   Explain why London is able to get a large part of its water supply from rocks below the city.   (3 marks)
(ii) Name two other major sources of water for the people of London.   (2 marks)

(c)   (i)   Name a highland area which is used to supply water for a major city.   (1 mark)
(ii) Name the city that the water is supplied to.   (1 mark)
(iii)Describe some of the other activities that often take place on and around water storage reservoirs.   (4 marks)

5 A Manufacturing industry

For this topic you should study:
- manufacturing industry as a system, with reference to:
  - inputs, processes and outputs
  - the influence of raw materials, fuel supplies, labour supply, transport, markets and government policy
  - a chemicals industry on a river estuary
  - modern industry along the M4 corridor.

Factors affecting industrial location

The simplest definition of manufacturing industry says that it 'takes raw materials and processes them to make finished products'. Really it is rather more complicated than this. Few factories take an item through the full process from raw material to finished product. Some factories use raw materials and process them. Then the product of that factory may be taken somewhere else to be made into parts, which are then used in an assembly plant to make finished products.

However, all factories have inputs which they process to produce outputs.

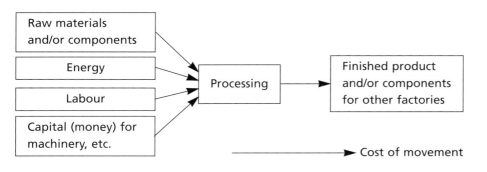

ocus Point 1

Cover up the diagram.

Name four types of input that go into any factory.

Give two names to describe the outputs of factories.

Every entrepreneur who builds a factory tries to choose the best possible site. This is the place where the factory can make most profit. One way of increasing profit is to increase sales, by being near a good market. Another way is to reduce costs. Geographers are especially interested in how costs can be reduced by cutting transport costs. Ways of reducing costs include building in or near to:

(1) mines, etc. which supply energy or raw materials

(2) railway stations, ports, motorway junctions, etc. where transport is cheaper

(3) areas with high unemployment, which have a cheaper labour force

(4) a well-trained labour force (cheaper training costs)

(5) areas where government subsidies are available (which are often areas of high unemployment)

(6) areas of dense population where there is a large market.

No location offers all the factors listed above, but different types of factory have different needs. For instance:

- An iron and steel works uses large amounts of iron ore and coal, so (1) would be very important for its location.

- A soft drinks canning plant does not use much raw material, because the main ingredient is water, so factor (1) is not important. However, the finished product is bulky, so it needs to cut transport costs for the finished product. Factor (6) is important.

In the two studies that follow – the chemicals industry and high-tech industry – you should keep the seven factors listed above in your mind at all times. They help to explain the very different location patterns of the two industries.

Hints and Tips!
Try to learn this list. You will probably not get a question that asks you to write out such a list, but it can provide a very good starting point for planning answers to questions on industrial location.

The chemicals industry on river estuaries
There are five river estuaries in the UK where major chemicals industries have developed. They are shown on the map to the right.

They all have the following features in common:

- They have easy access for large bulk-carrying ships.

- Oil refining has developed along each estuary.

- They all have flat, low-lying land on which to build large industrial complexes.

- They are well served by road transport.

- They are close to large urban areas which provide a labour force and a market.

However, the three more southerly areas have always relied almost completely on imported raw materials. Both Merseyside and Teesside originally developed because of local supplies of raw materials, and these are still important today.

Both areas are also near to coalfields which used to provide both energy and raw materials.

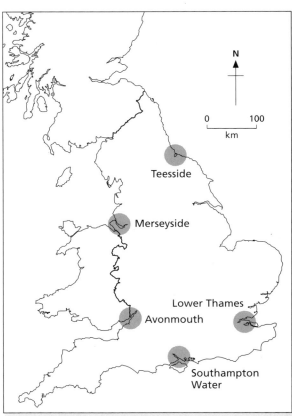

▲ *Major estuaries with chemicals industries*

The nature of modern chemicals industries
The chemicals industry in some areas has been described as resembling a 'spaghetti bowl'. The tangle of long strands of spaghetti is represented by the tangle of pipelines which connect the various plants.

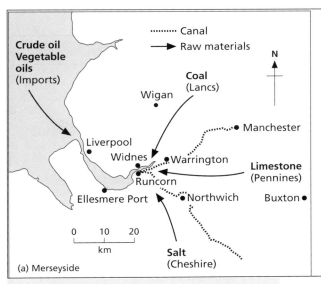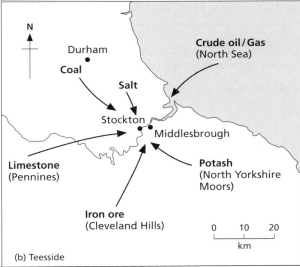

▲ *Raw materials for the chemicals industry*
(a) Merseyside   (b) Teesside

Essentially what happens in the modern chemicals industry is:

- raw materials consisting of complex chemical mixtures and compounds are taken and broken down
- different chemicals are separated from each other
- chemicals are reassembled to make new products.

The heavy chemicals industry uses large amounts of a few raw materials, and makes products for other industries. The light chemicals industry recombines those products into a variety of carefully designed products to meet precise market needs.

For instance, consider two products of the chemicals industry, plastics and pharmaceutical products (or medical drugs). Both come in an enormous range of products. Plastics can be clear or opaque, rigid or flexible, and biodegradable or non-biodegradable, and so on. Each special product is designed for a different purpose and needs a slightly different combination of the same chemical elements.

Pharmaceuticals are equally complex and varied. They range from common, rather old-fashioned drugs like aspirin and indigestion remedies to very sophisticated chemicals to treat cancers and AIDS or to prevent rejection of transplanted organs.

Hints and Tips!

There are many similarities between these two areas and Europort in the Netherlands (see Chapter 13). Study the two areas together. It makes it easier to learn all of them.

Why are Merseyside and Teesside good locations?

	Merseyside	Teesside
Access to raw materials	Local salt, limestone	Local salt, limestone, potash
Port facilities	Deepwater Mersey estuary.	Deepwater Tees estuary.
	Imports of oil etc.	Imports of oil etc. + pipelines from North Sea oil and gas fields.
Road links	M56, M6, M62 form a network around the area.	No motorway link to national motorway network but reasonable network of A roads.
Energy	Close to Lancashire coalfield. Used to be important, but now electricity provides main power.	Close to Durham coalfield. Used to be important. Now has gas-fired power stations, using North Sea gas.
Labour supply	High unemployment so cheap workforce is available.*	Long tradition of chemicals industry, so skilled workforce available.
Government incentives	Development areas, so aid available for building, equipping factories, training workers, tax reduction, etc.	
Capital	Local firms with long-standing links and investments in the area.	
Markets	Local textile and engineering industries provide markets. Easy access to Lancashire and Midlands conurbations. Local ports and airports for export.	Local engineering, mining industry etc. provides a market. Fairly easy access to Tyneside and Yorkshire conurbations. Local port and airport for export. Faces EU across North Sea

* Note that the chemicals industry is very capital intensive. It has a fairly small workforce compared with the large amount invested in capital and equipment. Most of the workforce are highly skilled and trained, so the presence of a cheap, unskilled workforce is not a very important factor.

High-technology industry in the M4 corridor

The raw materials used to make a computer are only worth a few pounds, but the actual cost of a computer may be well over a thousand pounds. The money pays for:

- the highly educated designers and programmers who developed the computer and its component parts, such as micro-chips and processors – in other words, **research and development (R&D)** costs

- the cost of developing the software

- the skilled labour that made the components, and then assembled them

- the cost of plant and machinery in the factories

- advertising and promotion

- transport of the very fragile finished product

- sales staff, and the after-sales technical back-up staff.

The Cambridge Science Park, linked to the university, is probably the UK's best example.

This all goes to show that the old rules of industrial location do not apply to modern, high-tech industry. Computer manufacture does not have to be located where the raw materials are imported, or near to a coal mine. Instead, industries like this are located in two types of area: the work is often split between 'development' sites and 'assembly' sites.

Development sites need:

- access to highly educated, creative thinkers, who are usually found in and around universities
- an attractive environment, where these workers will be willing to work
- contact with other people in high-tech industry, who can share ideas and stimulate further development work
- easy access to the rest of the world (via airports) so that ideas can be shared (potential buyers and providers of components and programs can easily keep in contact too)
- good road access, by fast, uncongested routes.

Assembly sites need:

- skilled and semi-skilled workers with reasonably low wage rates
- government subsidies (if possible) which are usually paid to firms that locate in 'development areas' with high unemployment
- easy contact with the development sites, and with the market – good road access is essential.

ocus Points 2 and 3

◆ Go through this list linking each point to a specific fact about the M4 Corridor on the map below. In other words, link the theory to a real-life example.

◆ Several assembly plants developed in small towns in South Wales and Central Scotland. Why were a lot of workers available here? Which declining industries had they come from?

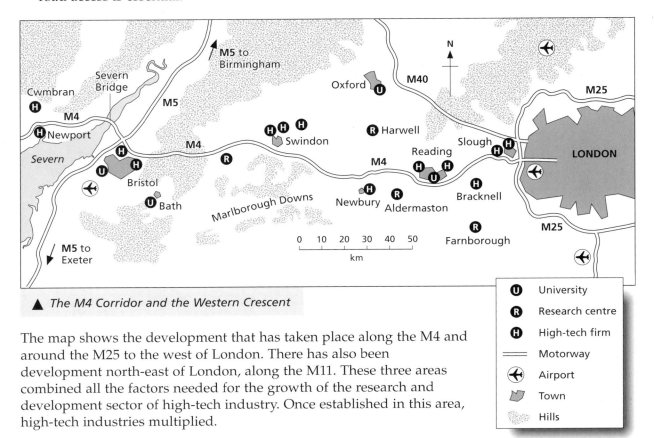

▲ The M4 Corridor and the Western Crescent

The map shows the development that has taken place along the M4 and around the M25 to the west of London. There has also been development north-east of London, along the M11. These three areas combined all the factors needed for the growth of the research and development sector of high-tech industry. Once established in this area, high-tech industries multiplied.

Questions

The M4 Corridor is also an important area for the development of the food processing industry.

1 Name a factory or food processing town that you have studied.

2 Describe the industry that has developed there.

3 Explain the factors that attracted it to that area.

Exam practice

Name a city in a less economically developed country that has attracted many new migrants.

(a) Explain why migrants have come to the city.
(Refer to push and pull factors.)   (6 lines 4 marks)

   (i) Give two reasons why industry often develops around river estuaries.   (2 marks)

   (ii) Name three river estuaries in the UK where large chemicals industries
have developed.   (3 marks)

(b) For one of the estuaries named in (a) (ii) above:

   (i) Name one raw material that is (or was) mined locally.   (1 mark)

   (ii) Name a place where that raw material was mined.   (1 mark)

   (iii) Name a raw material that is imported by ship.   (1 mark)

   (iv) Name a town close to the estuary where the chemicals industry is important.   (1 mark)

(c) Explain why many chemical plants are often found grouped close together in a
small area. Use examples to illustrate the points you make in your answer.   (5 marks)

(d) Why has the M4 Corridor developed as the main centre for high-tech industry
in the UK?   (6 marks)

5 B The changing pattern of retail trade and its location

For this topic you should study:
- the retail industry, with reference to:
  - the changing pattern of the retail industry and its location (out-of-town shopping centres and retail parks, and their effect on the high street
  - conflicting values and issues.

Out-of-town shopping centres v. CBDs

The central business district (CBD)
CBDs in most cities developed around the most accessible place. This was usually where several roads met, and near to railway and bus stations. When cities first started to grow there was usually a market place near the centre. The market place may still be there, but now most CBDs are dominated by offices and large shops.

- CBDs are very busy areas. This is because people can get to them easily from all directions.

- Because CBDs are accessible there are lots of customers for businesses located there.

- This makes businesses in this area very profitable so many firms want to locate in the CBD.

- Rents in CBDs are usually higher than in other parts of cities.

- All the businesses attract more and more customers to the CBD ... until the CBD is so congested that business starts to decline.

Hints and Tips!
In examinations you should usually avoid abbreviations, but 'CBD' is so common that it is safe to use it in geography.

ocus Point 1
Cover up this page and explain why rents of shops in CBDs are usually high.

Questions

For a case study city, draw a sketch map which shows:

- some routes into the CBD including some of the following: roads, railway lines, underground or metro lines, train and bus stations, major car parks, etc.
- the main shopping street(s), major department stores, pedestrian streets, or undercover shopping centres
- some of the main office areas
- other major features, such as a cathedral, football ground, town hall, etc.

Out-of-town shopping centres
The growth of out-of-town shopping centres has been very important during the last twenty years. They include the White Rose Centre (Leeds), Meadowhall (Sheffield), Merry Hill Centre in Dudley, Lakeside (next to the Dartford Crossing), and many others. What are the advantages of these centres that have led to their rapid growth?

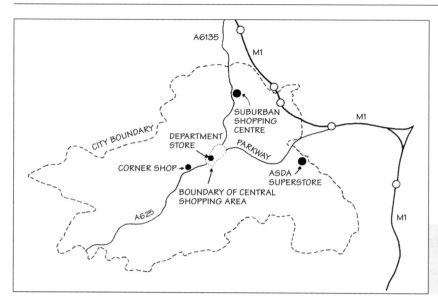

The development of out-of-town shopping centres would not have been possible without mass ownership of cars.

◀ *Shopping in the late 1970s From Melvyn Jones Assignment Geography, Nelson 1979*

• Land is cheaper on the edge of cities than in the CBDs.

• There is plenty of space for car parking. Stores that need a very large floor area have enough space to build on one level.

• New buildings can be put up without the costs of demolishing old ones, or fitting them around existing buildings.

• They are easily accessible by road, often being close to ring roads, by-passes and motorway interchanges.

The growth of out of town shopping produced a lot of competition for CBDs. In order to attract customers, many new developments were introduced into CBDs. These included:

• pedestrian streets, to make shopping pleasanter and safer

• pick-up points where shoppers can bring their cars close to the stores

• covered arcades and malls, to protect shoppers from the weather.

However, by about 1995, the out-of-town centres were falling out of favour with some people and organizations. What were the reasons for this change?

• Growth of new centres used up a lot of the countryside, threatening areas of green belt.

• Shops in city centres were threatened by the competition from out-of-town centres.

• New centres were only really accessible by car. This made it difficult for people without cars (the young, old, disabled, poor, single-parent families, etc.) to use them.

• Increased use of cars causes extra congestion, pollution, etc.

As a result, politicians and planners will probably bring in stricter rules to make it more difficult to develop out-of-town shopping centres.

Focus Point 2

Cover the page and write down four advantages of out-of-town shopping centres.

Hints and Tips!

Make a table with two headings 'Advantages...' and 'Disadvantages... of out-of-town shopping centres'. Complete the table by writing key words or short phrases in each column. This may be easier for you to learn than the full sentences used here.

Questions

1 Name an example of an out-of-town shopping centre that you have studied.

2 Draw a sketch map to show its location.

3 Label the sketch map to show why this was a good place to build.

4 Describe the market area of the centre. Either do this in words, or draw a map to show the area served by the development.

5 Has the growth of this centre affected trade in the CBD of the local town? If so, how?

Superstores v small shops

Superstores first appeared in the UK in the 1970s, and have grown in importance ever since. Now, four chain stores dominate the market for the household shopping: Tesco, Sainsburys, Asda and Safeway.

All these companies build big stores close to major roads, to attract people from a radius of up to about 15 miles. (This is less than the out-of-town centres, which attract people from a much larger area.) These stores sell a large volume of goods. They can offer low prices, and still make good profits because of this big turnover.

As time has passed the superstores have started to offer a bigger and bigger range of goods. This is very convenient for their customers, who can buy lots of different types of shopping at the same time. However, the growth of the superstores has put many small shops out of business, and threatens many others. For instance:

Superstores have a higher **threshold population** and a bigger **range** than corner shops. This means that they need to attract more people in order to make a profit, but because they offer good bargains people will travel further to shop at a superstore than they would travel to a corner shop.

Superstores sell:	This threatens the future of:
fresh vegetables	greengrocers and market stalls
fresh bread	bakers
newspapers	newsagents
beer and wine	off licences
medicines	chemists

Of course, most customers welcome the low prices and convenience, but as the superstores grow, corner shops, high street shops, village stores and many other services are disappearing. Once again, the less mobile lose out.

Hints and Tips!

In your exam you will be expected to show that you understand how people's different values and attitudes affect geographical decisions. This is a good topic for you to show that understanding. Be ready to explain why some groups can benefit from new shopping centres but other groups cannot use them easily.

Questions

1 Name a local superstore.

2 Describe its market area.

3 From your own knowledge, or by interviewing people who have known the area for longer than you, name any shops that have closed since the opening of the superstore.

4 Which groups of people benefit from the opening of superstores? Which groups lose out when local shops close? (Think about the rich and poor; young, middle-aged and elderly; car owners and public transport users; the disabled; single parents; and so on.)

5 Do superstores and out-of-town centres lead to an increase in road traffic and pollution?

6 Leisure and tourism

For this topic you should study:

- the Lake District National Park, with reference to:
  - the aims of the National Parks
  - the characteristics and major landform features of the Lake District, especially upland glaciation
  - the impact of tourism and second homes on the area
  - pressures such as erosion, conservation, conflicts of land use, and traffic
  - 'honeypot' sites (issues and possible solutions)

- the seaside holiday resort, with reference to:
  - distribution of resorts in relation to temperature and rainfall patterns and the distribution of population
  - causes and effects of changes in the resorts (amenity provision, extension of the season)

Leisure and tourism is one of the world's most rapidly growing industries. People in more economically developed countries have gained more leisure time and have more money to spend on leisure activities. This means that they are willing to pay people to provide services for them to enjoy in a variety of ways.

Leisure services become concentrated in particular areas – often in areas with specially attractive environments. In this syllabus, three particular environments are chosen for study. You must study coastal resorts in Mediterranean Spain, and these are covered in Chapter 11. The other two environments are in the UK:

- the National Parks, especially the Lake District

- seaside holiday resorts.

Remember, jobs in tourism are usually only seasonal. They cannot be relied on to offer a wage all year round.

The National Parks

There are eleven National Parks in England and Wales. The first National Parks in Britain were set up soon after the Second World War. They had two main aims:

To conserve areas of beautiful and remote countryside.	To encourage people to use these areas for leisure.

It should be clear that, right from the start, there was a potential conflict between these two aims, because:

One of the best ways to conserve the land, is to stop large numbers of people from using it.	If large numbers of people are encouraged to use the land they will almost certainly bring changes.

Another problem arose right from the start. The National Park Authorities do not own the land in the Parks. They just have responsibility for helping to plan how the land is used. In fact most of

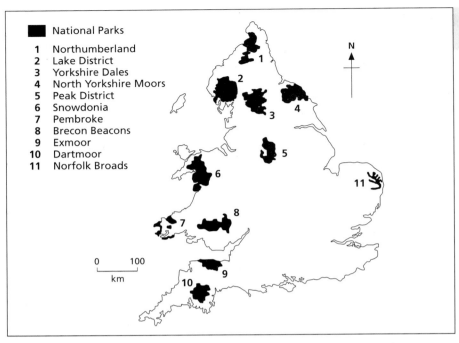

National Parks
1   Northumberland
2   Lake District
3   Yorkshire Dales
4   North Yorkshire Moors
5   Peak District
6   Snowdonia
7   Pembroke
8   Brecon Beacons
9   Exmoor
10 Dartmoor
11 Norfolk Broads

0   100
km

N

◀ *National Parks in England and Wales*

ocus Point 1

Cover up the map. Try naming all 11 National Parks. When you can name them all, try to mark them on a blank map of the UK.

ocus Point 2

Cover up the page. What are the two main aims of the National Parks?

What is the 'compromise' aim, which describes what the Park planners actually try to do?

the land is owned by farmers. Large areas are also owned by forestry companies, water boards, the National Trust, the Ministry of Defence, quarrying companies, private householders, etc. There could very easily be conflict between the needs of the land owners and the needs of people wanting to use the land for leisure. So the Park Authorities developed a new aim:

> To try to plan the use of the land so that the needs of all the potential users were met, and so that conflict between the different users was reduced as much as possible.

The Lake District National Park Authority has tried to do this by:

- setting up visitor information and education centres like the National Park Centre at Brockholes on the edge of Windermere

- introducing regulations to control some leisure activities, allowing them in certain areas and stopping them in others (e.g. allowing power boats on parts of Lake Windermere and Coniston, but banning them on other lakes, such as Wastwater)

- improving and maintaining footpaths, so that erosion caused by walkers does not get out of control

- signposting footpaths to help walkers, and to stop them wandering, getting lost, and damaging crops, walls and livestock

- controlling new building and alterations to existing buildings, by introducing strict rules about the type of materials and styles that can be used, and where building can take place.

You cannot understand the nature of tourism in the Lake District without studying the physical background to the area. This involves the study of glaciation and its effects.

Hints and Tips!

This is a list of key ideas (e.g. 'introducing regulations to control some leisure activities'). Try to learn these. In the exam you will earn more marks if you can elaborate the key ideas by giving an example or explanation, e.g. 'allowing power boats on parts of Lake Windermere and Coniston but banning them from Wastwater'.

Glaciation in the Lake District

The Ice Age in Britain lasted from about one million years BP (before the present) to about 20 000 BP. During this time there were several glacial periods, when temperatures fell and ice covered large parts of Britain, separated by inter-glacial periods. In fact, at the moment we may just be in a warm inter-glacial period before the next glaciation starts, and the ice advances again.

During a glacial period the temperature falls by 5–6°C. This means that more snow falls during the winter. In the highlands it does not all melt during the summer. Gradually the snow builds up and covers larger and larger areas with permanent snowfields.

Snow is made up of ice crystals, separated by large volumes of air. As the thickness of the snow cover increases, the lower layers are compressed by the weight above. This squeezes the air out and turns the snow into ice. This ice is much denser and harder than snow.

In some areas, after several decades of build-up of snow and ice, the weight can force the lower layers to start to move and flow out. In highland areas the flowing ice moves downhill, following the valleys. These 'rivers of ice' are called **glaciers**.

Erosion by ice

Before glaciers form there is a period of very cold weather when the rocks are weakened by **freeze–thaw weathering**. This weakens or shatters the rocks. Then the moving ice can erode the rocks in two ways.

◆ Imagine making a snowball. You take soft snow and squeeze it to make it firmer. By compressing it you squeeze out the air, and the ice crystals become more compact. This is similar to what happens when snow turns to ice in a glacier.

◆ When water freezes to form ice, its volume increases by about 10%. If water is trapped in cracks in rock this can put great pressure on the rock. After repeated freezing and thawing the rock may finally crack.

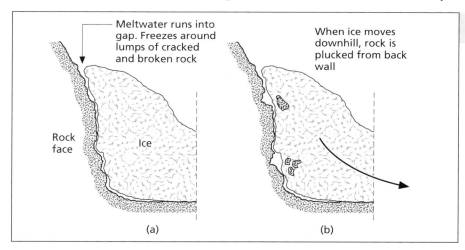

Meltwater runs into gap. Freezes around lumps of cracked and broken rock

When ice moves downhill, rock is plucked from back wall

Rock face

Ice

(a)

(b)

◀ Plucking

Hints and Tips!

Try to learn these diagrams. Practise drawing them so that you can draw them quickly and accurately in the exam. Examiners give a lot of credit for relevant, well-labelled diagrams.

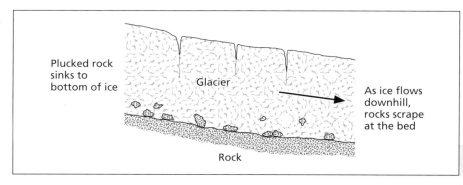

Plucked rock sinks to bottom of ice

Glacier

As ice flows downhill, rocks scrape at the bed

Rock

◀ Abrasion

These processes form particular physical features.

- **Corries** (called **cwms** in Wales and **cirques** in France) are deep hollows on a mountainside. They have a very steep back wall which is often partly covered by scree. They have a rounded or flat bottom, which may contain a small lake or tarn. There is often a rocky **lip**, where the glacier flowed out of the corrie.

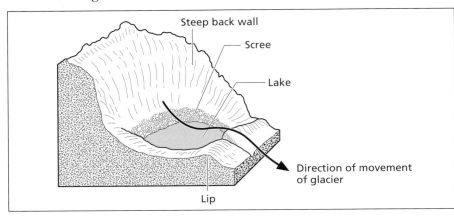

◀ *Cross-section of a corrie*

For example, on the side of Helvellyn in the eastern Lake District there are three large corries, all about 200 metres deep, called Brown Cove, Red Tarn and Nethermost Cove. (Red Tarn is the only one of the three that has a corrie lake.)

- **Arêtes** (or **knife-edge ridges**) are steep-sided ridges of land between two corries. The sides may fall for hundreds of metres, and the tops may be only one or two metres across.

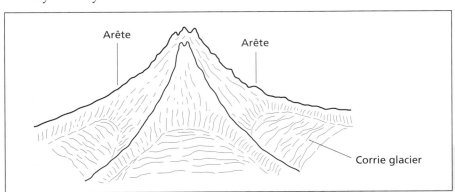

DID YOU KNOW ?

Some people describe corries as 'deep, armchair-shaped hollows'. If this phrase helps you to visualize a corrie, then remember it!

◀ *Arêtes between a group of corries*

On Helvellyn the arête between Brown Cove and Red Tarn is called Swirral Edge. The arête between Red Tarn and Nethermost Cove is called Striding Edge. It is very narrow and steep-sided and is one of the most exciting walks or scrambles in the area.

- **Glacial troughs** (or **U-shaped valleys**) are steep-sided, flat-bottomed valleys. They are usually fairly straight, because the glaciers which eroded them flowed straight, unlike rivers which meander. Some glacial troughs have long, narrow, **finger lakes** in them. These were formed mainly by the action of ice deepening the valleys, but also by moraine, deposited when the ice melted, which helped to dam some valleys.

ocus Point 4

Choose **either** a corrie **or** an arête **or** a U-shaped valley. Explain how plucking and abrasion helped to form your chosen feature.

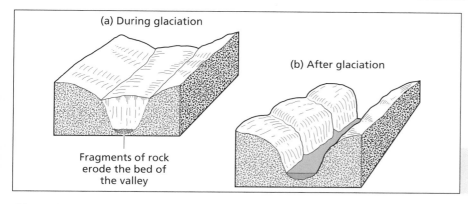

(a) During glaciation

Fragments of rock erode the bed of the valley

(b) After glaciation

◀ *U-shaped valley or glaciated trough*

Glenridding Valley and Grisedale lead from the corries on Helvellyn. They both join Ullswater which is the second longest finger lake in the Lake District (after Windermere.)

Questions

Learn the names of examples of the features listed above. Use the examples given, or ones that you have studied in class. You should be able to locate them on a map, and describe them.

The attractions of glaciated landscapes

- Most areas where glaciation starts are highlands. This is because temperatures are lower in highlands than in nearby lowlands.

- Highlands are also usually areas of hard rock because hard rock is resistant to erosion. Soft rocks are worn down to form lowlands.

- Because glaciers are mainly found in areas of high land, with hard rock, they produce spectacular scenery.

The valleys were made deep by the ice, but the land in between the valleys resists erosion and forms high peaks. The soil was scraped away from the high land by the ice, leaving the rock exposed, but even this rock is cracked and broken by ice action. This forms steep cliffs and jagged ridges, with flat green valleys in between.

The land in glaciated areas is wild and spectacular, and it attracts many people for outdoor leisure. Some come just to admire the scenery, but it also attracts walkers, rock climbers, skiers, hang-glider pilots, canoeists, mountain bikers, bird watchers, campers, and many others.

Unfortunately, so many people may be attracted that the wild, unspoilt scenery that attracted them may start to be damaged and spoilt!

Increased leisure time and mobility, and pressure on the Parks

Since the Second World War, people in Britain have more leisure time because:

- most working people now have longer periods of paid holiday

- most workers have a shorter working week than they used to

Hints and Tips!

You may be asked to give examples of how glaciated scenery is used for outdoor pursuits. Try to be precise. An answer that says 'Glaciated scenery can be used for walking' will gain some credit. One that says 'Glaciated scenery, like the Striding Edge arête on the side of Helvellyn, can be used for walking' will gain more marks.

- housework is less time-consuming because of labour-saving equipment.

People are also able to travel more easily because:

- far more families now have cars
- the road system has improved with the building of motorways
- networks of inter-city coaches now cover most of the country (although local bus services have declined in many areas).

In addition, the average person has far more 'disposable wealth' (spare money after essential costs have been paid). They have more money to spend on leisure. Many people in cities even have enough money to buy a second home or a caravan in the countryside, just for holiday use.

All this has put great pressure on the countryside, and the Lake District is one of the most seriously affected areas in the UK, because:

- The area has very beautiful scenery.
- It has always been fairly accessible from the densely populated conurbations of Lancashire, Yorkshire and Tyneside.
- The construction of the motorway network in the 1960s and 1970s, with the M6 running very close to the Lakes, made the area even more accessible to a larger number of people.
- The decline of employment in traditional Lakeland occupations like mining and hill farming left many houses abandoned and ready for conversion for tourism or second-home ownership. It also led to a need for diversification of employment, so tourist jobs were welcomed.

The development and management of 'honeypots'

Some of the most difficult problems for the planners in the Lakes have arisen at what are described as 'honeypot' sites. This name arose from the phrase 'they flock there like bees round a honeypot'. In the Lake District honeypots include:

- spectacular scenery for mountain walking, e.g. Helvellyn and the Langdale Pikes
- spectacular scenery accessible by car, e.g. Ashness Bridge near Keswick, and Tarn Hows
- literary links including Beatrix Potter's farm near Hawkshead, and Wordsworth's cottage in Grasmere
- attractive small towns, like Ambleside and Keswick, with their shops, cafés, hotels, museums, lakeside activities and so on
- other attractions, such as the Ravenglass and Eskdale railway and the National Park Centre at Brockholes.

Note that most of these examples have good road links. This is almost essential if a site is to develop into a honeypot. Even Helvellyn and the Langdale Pikes have seriously congested car parks in the valleys below them, and the footpaths to the summits are eroded by walkers.

DID YOU KNOW?

Of course some people in the UK still work very long hours and have very little leisure time.

Focus Point 5

You may well have visited or studied other honeypot sites. Where do they fit on this list?

Hints and Tips!

This list is an attempt to classify honeypot sites. Putting them in groups like this is a way of making learning easier, and of helping to give a structure to exam answers.

When a site becomes a honeypot, many problems can result, but the tourists can also bring benefits to the local area.

Problems	Benefits
• Litter. • Lack of parking spaces, and spread of parked cars onto verges, farmland, etc. • Road congestion in the neighbourhood. • Lack of toilets. • Overuse of footpaths leading to erosion of land surface.	• Trade for local shops. • Money provided for investment in roads, etc • Jobs for local people. • Farmers can sell produce such as eggs to visitors. • Conflict with farmers because of tourists damaging hedges, gates, etc. • Spare farm buildings can be converted into holiday cottages. • B & B guests can be taken in

Questions

1 Give an example of a honeypot location that you have studied.

2 Describe its attractions.

3 Describe the problems caused by its overuse.

4 Discuss some possible management solutions.

Focus Point 6

Choose one of the honeypot types listed here, or one of your own examples. Make two lists: people who benefit from the existence of the honeypot, and those who suffer.

The problem of second homes

In the past, people who lived in villages worked, shopped and carried out their social lives there. The traditional village had a pub, a church, a village hall and a few shops, including a post office and general store. There also had to be a bus service to the local town, because there were not enough people to support a full range of services in the village.

All this changed as the number of second homes and holiday cottages increased. Many houses in the villages are now only lived in at weekends or during the summer; for much of the year they are empty. Meanwhile young people who were born in the village often cannot find work there, or cannot afford to buy homes there because people with jobs in the cities can pay much higher prices for the houses. As house prices increase, local people are forced out and often have to rent council houses in nearby towns.

Local shops and services also suffer from this change. Second-home owners often shop in the city, where prices are much cheaper, so local shops lose trade. Of course they may increase their sales of tourist goods but they can no longer provide the full range of food and household goods. Meanwhile the church, the pub and the village hall lose congregations and customers as the resident population shrinks.

Even the local people come to rely on the town for shopping. More of them have cars and so the bus services lose passengers. In many cases it is only the young, the old and the poor who need to use buses. The number of fare-payers declines, so services are cut. People without cars become more isolated and village life gets more difficult, forcing yet more people to leave.

In the Lake District an attempt has been made to boost public transport by setting up 'post buses'. The postmen who visit the villages use mini-buses and take fare-paying passengers into the towns, but this can only provide a very basic and irregular service at best. Villages continue to lose their services and their sense of identity. The newcomers conserve and improve the houses, but cannot conserve the communities.

Questions

Name and describe a village that has been much affected by the growth of second-home ownership.

The British seaside holiday resort

The fashion for taking holidays by the sea started in the late eighteenth and early nineteenth centuries, but only the aristocracy and the very rich had enough time and money to take holidays. It was not until the late nineteenth and early twentieth centuries that ordinary working people could take holidays. Two changes led to the growth of seaside resorts in Britain.

- The building of railways from industrial towns to the resorts allowed people to travel to the seaside for the first time.

- Employers began to allow their workers to take paid holidays.

Until the 1950s many holidaymakers travelled only as far as their local resorts. As car ownership became more common, from the 1960s onwards, and as people had longer holidays, they could travel farther

People sometimes accuse shops in little tourist villages of charging prices that are far too high. However, they have to do this because the tourist season is only short and the shopkeeper has to make enough profit to survive during the winter.

The tourist industry has always depended on fashion. In England, resorts like Bognor Regis and Lyme Regis took advantage of visits by the king. They gained publicity by adding 'Regis' (Latin for 'King') to their original names.

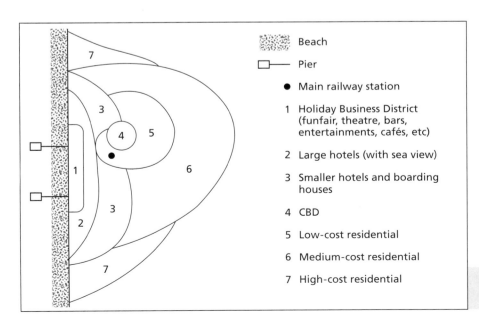

Beach

Pier

● Main railway station

1 Holiday Business District (funfair, theatre, bars, entertainments, cafés, etc)

2 Large hotels (with sea view)

3 Smaller hotels and boarding houses

4 CBD

5 Low-cost residential

6 Medium-cost residential

7 High-cost residential

◀ *A model of the British seaside resort*

for their holidays. There was a steady growth of resorts on the south coast, as people travelled further for better weather.

Holidaymakers in Britain can never rely on good weather. Resorts in the UK had to develop alternative attractions that could be used in the dull, wet weather that often occurs here in summer. Councils built funfairs, piers, theatres, zoos, aquariums and a variety of other facilities for indoor leisure.

These resorts developed a clear pattern of urban structure, similar in some ways to the models of ordinary towns, but with extra functions added. In most resorts the area close to the sea-front was dominated by large, expensive hotels. As distance from the front increased, the size and cost of holiday accommodation fell.

British resorts were hit by the growth of package holidays from the 1960s onwards. These developed as cheap air fares became available and massive investments were made around the Mediterranean. The resorts could almost guarantee summer sunshine, and prices could be kept low because of lower wage rates there.

In order to compete and to try to preserve jobs and profits, British holiday resorts had to develop many new strategies to attract customers. In addition to the indoor facilities these included:

- illuminations in the autumn to extend the season

- conference facilities to bring in political parties, trade unions, large firms etc. to stay in the hotels and use the resorts' facilities

- cheap weekend breaks and 'theme' holidays to encourage people to take a second holiday in addition to their main holiday abroad

- special Christmas, Valentine and Easter packages to extend the season.

Low wage rates in many Mediterranean countries mean that it is still cheaper to go on holiday there even though tourists have to pay for the cost of their flight. See Chapter 11.

Questions

Choose a British seaside resort that you have studied.

1 Describe its climate.

2 Did it develop to serve a local population, or has it always relied on people travelling from other parts of the country?

3 Can you identify areas in the resort like those shown on the model above?

4 What special attractions have been developed to attract customers in summer and to extend the holiday season?

Exam practice

(a) Give the two main aims of the National Parks when they were first set up.   (1 mark)

(b) (i)   Name one feature in the Lake District that was formed by glacial erosion.   (1 mark)
    (ii) Describe the feature.   (2 marks)
    (iii) Explain how it was formed. You may use a diagram to help your
          explanation.   (5 marks)

(c) (i)   What is a 'honeypot' site?   (1 mark)
    (ii) Name an example of a honeypot site in the Lake District.   (1 mark)
    (iii) Describe two problems caused by visitors to honeypot sites and the areas
          around them.   (4 marks)

(d) Choose a seaside holiday resort in the UK.
    (i)   Mark and name that resort on an outline map of the UK.   (1 mark)
    (ii) Holiday resorts in the UK have to compete with resorts around the
          Mediterranean which have a more reliable summer climate. Describe some
          of the attractions that your named resort has provided:
          • to attract holidaymakers in summer
          • to extend the holiday season beyond the summer.   (4 marks)

7 Ports

For this topic you should study:
- reasons for the growth and decline of ports
- the increased importance of east coast locations
- the effects of EU membership on trade
- changes such as bulk carriers, roll on/roll off facilities, use of containers and the effect of these on the distribution of trade
- cross-Channel traffic.

Everyone knows that a port is a place where ships come in to land and to load and unload. They do not always remember that it is also the place where land transport meets the ships and loads and unloads. The docks are a vital part of the port, but the railway sidings, the lorry parks, the warehouses and so on are equally important. The flow diagram shows the traffic moving one way, but it moves the other way too.

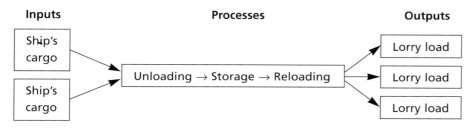

As cargoes are unloaded, stored and reloaded, it is often convenient to do other work on them too. Loading and unloading adds handling costs, so it is more economic to process raw materials before they are distributed around the country. Therefore industry often develops in ports.

Liverpool was typical of a port where industry developed. In addition to the cargo handling there was a lot of employment in shipbuilding and repairing, trade, insurance of ships and cargoes, and many other sectors. It imported many raw materials that led to the development of local industry.

The area inland that is served by the port is called its **hinterland**. Read exactly what this means in relation to Rotterdam, on page 87.

Import	from	Used for
Cane sugar	West Indies	Sugar refining, jam, sweets
Wheat	USA and Canada	Flourmilling, cakes, etc.
Palm oil	West Africa	Soap and margarine
Crude oil	Middle East	Petrol and chemicals

Unfortunately for Merseyside, many of these industries and the shipbuilding and repairing that served the port, have now declined or even disappeared. There are several reasons for this decline.

- **Trade with North America and other markets decreased as trade with EU increased**
  - cane sugar imports were replaced by home-grown sugar beet
  - North American wheat was replaced by wheat from the EU
  - palm oil was replaced by UK and EU oils, such as rape-seed oil.

- **Decline in exports**
  - the Lancashire cotton industry declined
  - more of the UK's exports go to the EU from east coast ports.

- **Port facilities moved from the city centre docks** because:
  - new greenfield sites developed with modern cargo-handling facilities
  - they thus avoided city centre road congestion.

- **There were changes in technology**
  - bulk carriers, container ships etc. can carry more goods, more cheaply
  - more efficient ways of lifting goods off the ships and transferring them to road or rail transport. These include:
    - roll on/roll off facilities
    - cranes to lift containers straight from ship to lorry or train
    - automatic unloading of bulk carriers.

Hints and Tips!

This section on declining ports contains four main headings and a number of sub-headings. The information is broken down like this to help you to **structure** your knowledge. This should make your revision easier. It also gives you a ready-made plan which you can use in any exam answer on this topic.

This new technology came to ports in the UK in the 1960s and 1970s. It brought great benefits but it also caused very serious problems in old dockland areas like Liverpool.

Benefits include:	Problems include:
• Ships can be unloaded more quickly.	• Many dock workers lost their jobs, especially older, less skilled men.
• Goods can be delivered to their destination faster and more reliably.	• Many buildings and docks were abandoned, leaving ugly, dangerous areas.
• There are fewer breakages and less damage to goods.	• People with jobs in the new docks often moved out of old dockland areas.
• Hard, dangerous work was replaced by machinery.	• As people with good jobs moved out, the old areas were left with fewer people earning good wages.
• Some low-paid workers can be trained for better, higher-paid work.	• Shops and businesses in the area lost customers and often had to close

Many old dockland areas went into a downward spiral. Jobs and services were lost, the environment got worse, crime increased, and people lost hope. However, much has now been done to try to revitalize old dockland areas. The redevelopment of London Docklands is probably the most famous example, but the Liverpool docks have been changed enormously too. New initiatives have included:

- Merseyside Garden Festival, which reclaimed and landscaped a lot of the old riverside area

- Albert Dock redevelopment, where old warehouses have been converted into flats, leisure facilities, offices, art galleries and so on.

ocus Point 1

Cover up the page. List four advantages of the new port technology. List four problems that the growth of new technology caused in the old ports.

Growth of the east coast ports

As the west coast ports have declined, those in the east and south-east have grown. The reasons are summarized on the map below.

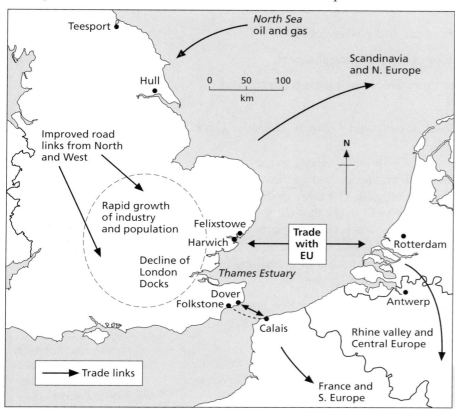

Map labels:
- Teesport
- North Sea oil and gas
- Hull
- Scandinavia and N. Europe
- 0 50 100 km
- N
- Improved road links from North and West
- Rapid growth of industry and population
- Felixstowe
- Harwich
- Trade with EU
- Rotterdam
- Decline of London Docks
- Thames Estuary
- Dover
- Folkstone
- Antwerp
- Calais
- Rhine valley and Central Europe
- Trade links
- France and S. Europe

Growth of the east coast ports

Hints and Tips!

It might be interesting to compare what happened as Liverpool docks declined with what happened in the Ruhr region as coal mining declined (see page 73). The Ruhr had serious problems too, but more careful plans were made there to try and reduce the effect of job losses and damage to the environment.

Dover is a good example of a port that has grown rapidly during the last 40 years but its future is now under threat. Both the growth and the threat have been caused by a combination of new technology and changes in the UK's relationship with Europe.

How new technology helped Dover to grow

- Roll on/roll off ('ro-ro') terminals allowed lorries to drive straight on and off ships without needing to load and unload their contents.

- Development of containers and specialized cranes speeded up handling of cargo.

- Newer, larger ferries allowed faster, smoother sea crossings and this attracted more customers.

- Better navigation techniques allowed crossings to continue in almost all weather conditions.

How changes in the UK's relationship with Europe helped Dover to grow

- Membership of the EU increased the UK's links with Europe.

- Reduction of customs barriers encouraged trade with the EU.

- Closer contacts with EU countries encouraged more visits by holidaymakers, school parties, business people, etc.

Hints and Tips!

Much of the trade from the east coast ports goes into Europe through Rotterdam. Many of the ideas in this section are very similar to those relating to Rotterdam in Chapter 13. You might revise more efficiently if you study these two chapters together.

How new technology threatens Dover's future growth

- The main threat comes in the form of the Channel Tunnel. This has already caused:

  – a reduction in the number of lorries using Dover port

  – a slowing in the growth of car and passenger traffic

  – a reduction in the number of ferries using the port

  and two of the main ferry companies have merged to try and compete with the Tunnel.

How changes in the UK's relationship with Europe threaten Dover's future growth

- At present people crossing the Channel by ferry can buy duty-free products. They can buy alcohol, cigarettes and perfumes cheaply because no customs duties are charged. The ferry operators make a good profit on these sales. Now the EU says that duty-free sales should not be allowed on ferries between two EU ports. If this ban goes ahead the ferry companies will lose a lot of income. They may have to raise their fares or reduce the number of crossings. Either of these changes will mean a loss of jobs in Dover.

- The EU is also reducing the need for passports when people travel between member states. If fewer passport checks and customs checks are needed, this could mean job losses in Dover.

- As trade between the UK and Europe grows there seems to be an increase in industrial action aimed at the Channel ports. Dover can be badly hit by strikes and blockades in France.

However, it seems that these threats are not likely to stop Dover's growth. They may slow the growth down, but the east coast ports are likely to go on growing as the UK develops closer links with Europe.

Questions

Choose a port on the east coast of England.

1 Describe the site of its dock area.

2 Describe its situation, or its links with the rest of this country and its trade partners.

3 Explain how its trade has developed over the last 30 years or so, giving clear reasons for the change.

The main reason for much of this new technology is to reduce the labour force needed to load and unload ships. This reduces costs, which means that prices can be cut and profits increased.

The fire in the Channel Tunnel in 1997 did cause serious disruption to its operations. It also made many people worried about its safety. This helped Dover, because it increased the number of ferry-users, but it seems likely that people will go back to the Tunnel when they feel reassured that it is safe.

Focus Point 2

Do you think that Dover will continue to grow? Cover up the page, and then give reasons for your answer to this question.

Exam practice

(a) (i)   Name a port in the UK that has suffered a fall in its trade during the
last 50 years.   (1 mark)

   (ii)   Give two reasons to explain why its trade has fallen.   (4 marks)

(b) Choose a port on the east or south-east coast of England that has seen an
increase in its freight traffic in recent years.

   (i)   Mark and name that port on an outline map of the UK.   (1 mark)

   (ii)   Explain why its geographical situation has helped to cause the increase
in its trade.   (4 marks)

   (iii)   How is your chosen port linked to its hinterland?   (1 mark)

   (iv)   Describe some of the cargo-handling facilities that have made the port
attractive to companies importing and exporting freight.   (4 marks)

(c) (i)   Name a port that has an important ferry service for cross-Channel
passengers, and cars.   (1 mark)

   (ii)   How is the passenger trade of the port likely to be affected by:
• increased use of the Channel Tunnel
• abolition of duty-free sales on ferries?   (4 marks)

8 Road transport

For this topic you should study:

- the importance of road transport
- effects of increased accessibility and problems of overuse
- advantages and disadvantages of road development (values and issues)
- motorway routes in relation to relief, centres of industry and population
- links with ports, the Channel Tunnel and continental Europe.

The increase in road transport

The tables below show how the traffic carried in the United Kingdom, by various forms of transport, changed over a 26-year period from 1966 to 1992.

Passenger transport (billion vehicle km)						
	Car	Bus	Train	Cycle	Air	Total
1966	175	70	30	20	–	295
1976	300	60	15	5	5	365
1986	450	45	15	–	10	520
1992	560	45	15	–	15	635

Freight transport (billion tonne km)					
	Road	Rail	Water*	Pipeline	Total
1966	70	20	25	–	115
1976	110	15	15	5	145
1986	120	20	30	15	185
1992	160	15	30	25	230
*= canal and coastal shipping					

The tables above show that there has been a massive increase in road transport over the last quarter of a century. That increase is still going on. Movement of passengers more than trebled over the period, and movement of freight by road more than doubled. In 1950 only 14 per cent of households in the UK had a car. Now almost 70 per cent have at least one car, and more than 25 per cent have two or more cars!

Note that there were not massive losses for most other forms of transport over the same period, but the huge increase in the total movement was mainly accounted for by increased use of cars and lorries.

The pattern of major road routes

The pattern of routes develops as a balance between two sets of influences. There are positive factors which attract roads and traffic to certain areas. There are also negative factors which make road building difficult and expensive and which repel traffic from some areas. The table below shows some of these factors:

ocus
Point 1

Complete the 'Total' columns on the two tables.

How has the total movement of passengers and freight changed over this period?

How has the importance of road transport for the movement of passengers changed over the period?

How has the importance of road transport for the movement of freight changed in the same period?

Hints and Tips!

You could say 'Road transport gained an increasing share of a growing market'.

Positive factors (which attract roads and traffic)	Negative factors (which repel roads and traffic)
• Large concentrations of people • Industrial areas • Ports, airports and rail terminals • Sport, culture and entertainment venues • Shopping and trade centres	• High land and steep slopes • River estuaries and deep valleys • Marshy and unstable land • Industrial dereliction • Mining subsidence

Two of the most important influences are **relief** and **population**.

● Dense population attracts road builders, because large concentrations of people need roads and are willing to pay for them.

● High relief is definitely a negative factor which puts off road builders because it makes road building expensive. (Note that high relief usually also deters settlement – few people live in high areas so there is not much need for roads there.)

The map shows the main motorways in the UK There is a strong negative correlation between the presence of high land and the presence of motorways. The M62 between Lancashire and Yorkshire is the only major exception to this negative relationship. There is a strong positive correlation between dense population and motorways.

Focus Point 2

Study the course of the M1. Does it avoid areas of negative factors? Is it attracted to areas with positive factors?

Study the course of the M62. Why does it go through an area which has very strong negative factors for road building?

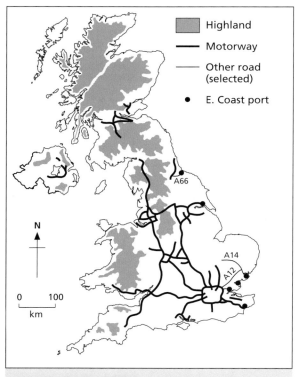

▲ *The UK's motorway network*

Legend:
- Highland
- Motorway
- Other road (selected)
- E. Coast port

A66
A14
A12

N
0   100
km

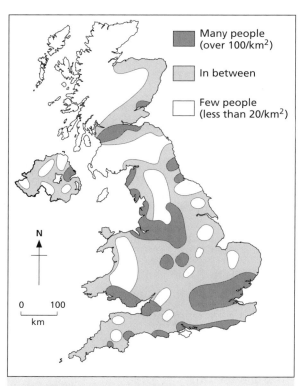

▲ *Population density in the UK*

Legend:
- Many people (over 100/km²)
- In between
- Few people (less than 20/km²)

N
0   100
km

Questions

The east coast ports studied in Chapter 7 are shown on the map above and marked *. Choose one of these ports. Describe how it is linked to its market area or hinterland by the road network.

Benefits of increased road transport

In many surveys transport users have been asked to compare motor transport with other forms of transport. The overwhelming response is always that road transport is far more convenient. People can travel from door to door and are not tied by timetables. The road network is more extensive than any other, and this increases the flexibility of cars and lorries. People often add that, although driving is sometimes stressful, it can also be enjoyable.

There are several benefits brought by increased road usage.

- **Growth of commuting** People can live in attractive areas outside cities, and still have well-paid jobs in the city.

- **Increase of out-of-town shopping, hypermarkets, etc.** These rely on road transport for deliveries, and cars for their customers.

- **Decentralization of industry** – including the move away from city centre/port/railway terminal/raw material locations to greenfield, out-of-town sites, which are less polluted and congested.

- **Greater flexibility of leisure** More people are able to take short holidays, trips to the seaside and countryside, visit sporting events, etc.

Questions

Take each of the points listed above. Name a place that you have studied which could be used as a case study to illustrate each point.

Problems caused by road transport

As well as benefits, cars have caused many problems. For instance they lead to:

- many deaths and injuries to people and wildlife

- air pollution that can help cause
  - asthma and other lung diseases
  - acid rain, from the release of sulphur dioxide from exhausts
  - the greenhouse effect, from the release of carbon dioxide

- stress due to noise which constantly affects some people living close to main roads

---

Hints and Tips!

Be sure that you could write about the influence of road transport on your main case study (or studies) of urban geography in the UK.

Hints and Tips!

Refer to Chapter 1 for greater detail on the effects of road transport on the structure of towns in the UK.

Hints and Tips!

Refer to Chapter 5 for greater details on the effects of road transport on the location of industry in the UK.

Hints and Tips!

Refer to Chapter 5 for greater details on the effects of road transport on the location of retail activities in the UK.

Attempts to reduce problems of cars in towns

- One bus can carry as many people as 20 cars, so use of buses cuts down congestion and pollution. Many councils try to encourage the use of buses by park-and-ride schemes, bus priority lanes, increasing the price of car parking, subsidizing bus routes, etc.

- Commuter railway systems and tramways have been re-introduced in many cities, although the capital costs of building them are high (e.g. Tyneside Metro, Sheffield Supertram).

Cambridge City Council is considering plans to keep cars out of the city centre. Plans have also been made which could possibly lead to charges for motorists who enter Central London.

Questions

1 Name a town where you have studied the problems of traffic.

2 Describe the problems and say where they are found.

3 Describe some of the attempts that have been made to tackle the town's transport problems.

Exam practice

(a) Imagine that you are a salesperson who works for a soft drinks company. You visit schools in an area that stretches about 50 miles around your office to sell them supplies for their drinks vending machines. Your boss thinks you should use public transport – buses and trains – to do your travelling. Explain why a car would be more efficient and more convenient.   (4 marks)

(b) Road transport damages the environment. Describe two different types of environmental damage caused by:

   (i) building roads
   (ii) increasing traffic on roads.   (4 marks)

(c) **Either** Choose an area in the United Kingdom where there are no motorways, or where there are very few motorways. Explain why no/few motorways have been built in your chosen area.

   Or Choose an area in the United Kingdom where there is a dense network of motorways. Explain why the dense network has developed in that area.   (5 marks)

(d) Some towns and cities have problems of traffic congestion in central areas. Choose a town or city where planners are attempting to reduce the problems of traffic congestion.

   (i) Describe one or more schemes that they have introduced, or are planning to introduce.
   (ii) Explain how the scheme will reduce the problem of traffic congestion.   (7 marks)

The European Union

9 Farming in southern Italy

For this topic you should study:
- traditional methods of agriculture
- responses to environmental constraints (relief, climate, soils)
- land reform and associated infrastructure changes – successes and failures.

Italy is a long, narrow peninsula which sticks out into the Mediterranean Sea. Physically there are four main regions:

- the Alps in the North
- the Piedmont, a flat, fertile, alluvial plain to the south of the Alps
- the Apennines, a range of young volcanic mountains
- the coastal plain.

The word **peninsula** comes from two Latin words. *Insula* means 'island'. When *pen'* is put in front of a word it means 'almost'. So a peninsula is a piece of land with sea on three sides of it. In other words, it is 'almost an island'.

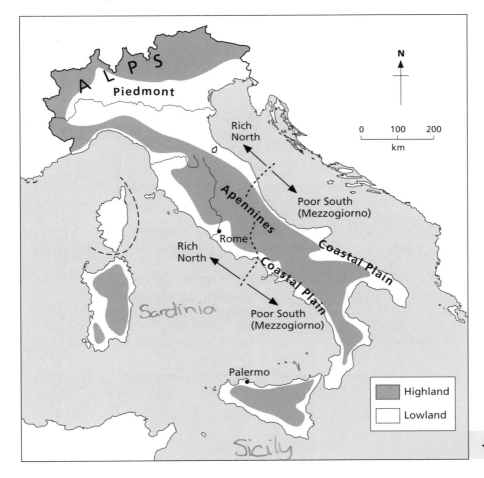

◀ *Regions of Italy*

Economically there are two main regions:

- the North, which is rich and developed
- the South or Mezzogiorno, which is poor and far less developed.

Physical conditions for farming in the South

The climate of the Mezzogiorno is typical of the Mediterranean climate region (see 'Mediterranean climate' in Chapter 11).

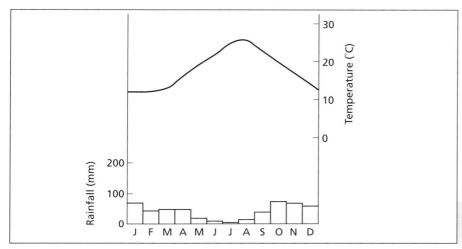

Climate of Palermo (see map page 68)

The relief is very broken. Some of the mountains in the main fold ranges rise to almost 3000 metres. The volcano, Mt Etna, is the highest point in the South and is (at present!) 3340m high.

Most of the land is between 200 and 1500m high, with many small ranges of hills. These are separated by deep, steep-sided valleys with fast-flowing streams eroding rapidly into the newly uplifted land. The flood plains of these rivers are rarely very large, so there is little flat land for building or agriculture. Instead, farmers have to cultivate the steep slopes and the hill tops. In many areas they have cut terraces into the hillsides to try and increase the amount of level land.

On the steep slopes soils are usually very thin because:

- water runs off easily because of the slope
- in summer most rain that falls comes in torrential downpours, encouraging fast run-off
- vegetation cover is often poor because it has been grazed by sheep and goats. This also allows fast run-off, and means there are few roots to hold the soil in place
- shortage of flat land means that land that is quite steep is ploughed. This can loosen soil and allow it to be washed away easily.

In these difficult conditions an almost **feudal**[1] system (often called *latifundia*) was still found in large parts of southern Italy at the end of the war in 1945. There were three distinct areas.

[1]'Feudal' means that a few powerful people owned most of the land. They allowed tenants to use some of it, but the poor farmers had very few rights on the land they farmed.

Hints and Tips!
Learn to draw a quick sketch map of Italy. Mark on the border between the North and the Mezzogiorno. Then mark on the Apennines and the coastal plain in the South. You do not need to learn the details about the North.

ocus Point 1

The Mediterranean climate has:

- Hot dry summers
- East winds
- Warm wet winters
- West winds.

Select figures from the graph that illustrate temperature and rainfall in both summer and winter.

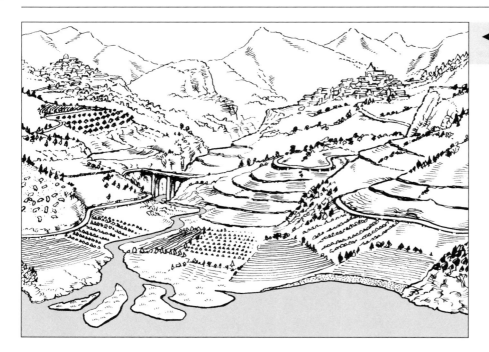

◀ *The landscape of southern Italy*

Focus Point 2

Cover the page. Give two reasons to explain why there is so little flat farmland in southern Italy.

Give three reasons why the soils are so thin.

On the coastal plain, where the land is flatter and soils are better, there were some large estates. Parts of these estates were used for growing grapes, olives, citrus fruits and tobacco for commercial purposes. Other areas were rented to peasant farmers to grow subsistence crops of wheat and fruit, and to keep some animals, especially sheep and goats.

Many of the landlords lived away from the area, in the cities, and paid very little attention to their land. Little money was invested in most of the estates so farming methods were backward. It was difficult to sell any surplus crops because of the distance to the big markets in northern Italy. Roads between North and South were poor.

Inland, most of the higher, steeper land was rented to peasants for subsistence farming. They grew wheat on patches of flat land scattered around the area, often at a distance of several kilometres from the villages. Vegetables were grown on small plots near the villages. Each family usually owned one or two olive trees and a small area of vines, and had a few sheep or goats which grazed on the poorest land.

In the highest mountains the land was mainly used for grazing sheep and goats, which destroyed much of the vegetation.

The Cassa per il Mezzogiorno

In 1950 the Cassa was set up to improve conditions in the South. The area was poor and backward in many ways. Income levels were much lower than in the North; there was little industrial employment; and migration from South to North was taking place on a huge scale. When the Cassa was first set up the Italian government provided £600 million for development work, and the World Bank gave over £250 million. In the first ten years the Cassa spent its funds as follows.

Note Because the farmers did not own their own land it was not worth them investing in improvements to the land – they could be forced off the land if their landlord wished. The lack of education also meant that the farmers tended to keep to the traditional ways of farming.

56% went on farming improvements

- The Cassa took over land from the big absentee landlords and broke it up into small plots which were given to families to farm. They received enough land to be self-sufficient:
  - 5 hectares if the land was good and could be irrigated
  - more than 5 hectares if it could not be irrigated
  - less than 5 hectares if they already had some land, or another job.

- Small farmers were given cheap loans for farm improvements.

- Agricultural colleges were set up to improve skills.

- Reforestation schemes and river control schemes were introduced to slow down soil erosion and stop flooding.

20% went on infrastructure particularly:

- roads linking rural areas to towns, and the South to the North

- water supply, for domestic use and to improve irrigation

- electricity supply, which also helped the farmers.

24% went on industrial development, education, health care, etc.

By 1960 the investment had improved agriculture, but people were still leaving the South in large numbers. Unemployment was still high. Since then the Cassa has invested funds in trying to develop industry and tourism to:

- increase employment opportunities

- increase the local market for agricultural produce.

Much of the money for development in the region now comes from the European Union. The **Integrated Mediterranean Programme (IMP)** tries to modernize farming throughout the southern part of the EU.

40% of the budget goes directly to farming to:

- improve the quality of olive and vine growing

- improve animal care, especially through better veterinary care

- improve marketing organizations.

33% of the budget goes to creating off-farm jobs such as craft activities, small-scale industry, small hotels, campsites, etc.

27% of the budget goes to:

- improving fishing by modernizing ports and buying new boats

- extending forestry and reducing soil erosion

- education and training.

Unfortunately the amount of money for the IMP is small when compared with the size of the Common Agricultural Policy (CAP). The

ocus Point 3

Cover the page. Up to 1960, how did the Cassa spend its money? List:
- three ways it invested in agriculture
- three ways it invested in infrastructure
- three other developments it invested in.

Why does the Cassa mainly invest in industry now?

Hints and Tips!

Make sure you can remember the names 'Cassa' and 'Integrated Mediterranean Programme' (or at least remember IMP).

CAP pays subsidies to farmers based on the quantity they produce. It does not encourage them to grow high-quality produce needed by the market. This means there is still far too much land growing low-quality crops of tobacco, olives, wine and wheat. These are not needed but are bought by the CAP, and kept in store.

Unless the CAP is modernized soon it will go on supporting poor, old-fashioned farming. In addition, the complex structure of subsidies means that illegal organizations can cheat the system. This means that illegal organizations such as the Mafia are still strong, and this all acts to discourage modernization.

ocus Point 4

The IMP invests in:
- improving farming
- off-farm jobs
- other projects.

List three ways money is spent on each of these programmes.

Exam practice

(a) (i)   On an outline map of Italy, mark the boundary of the Mezzogiorno region.   (1 mark)

   (ii)   Write a brief description of the climate of southern Italy. Refer to temperature and rainfall conditions in summer and winter.   (4 marks)

   (iii)   Why does the relief of southern Italy often make farming difficult?   (3 marks)

   (iv)   Many farmers in southern Italy are 'largely subsistence farmers'. What does this phrase mean?   (1 mark)

   (v)   Why is access to the market a problem for many farmers in southern Italy?   (2 marks)

(b) (i)   What is the Cassa per il Mezzogiorno?   (1 mark)

   (ii)   Describe one of its policies.   (2 marks)

   (iii)   What is the Integrated Mediterranean Programme (IMP)?   (1 mark)

   (iv)   Describe one of its policies.   (2 marks)

(c)   To what extent have the Cassa per il Mezzogiorno and the IMP been successful in raising the standard of living in southern Italy?   (3 marks)

10 The Ruhr conurbation and industrial change

For this topic you should study:
- the rise and decline of coal mining
- the changing nature of manufacturing
- settlement, planning and the environment
- the work of the Ruhr Planning Authority.

The growth and decline of heavy industry

The Ruhr industrial conurbation is built on the coalfield which lies beneath the North German Plain, mostly to the east of the River Rhine. In the 1930s this region was described as 'the workshop of Western Europe'. Its main industries were:

- coal mining
- steel making (using the coal and imported iron ore)
- heavy engineering (using local steel and powered by locally mined coal).

The manufacture of chemicals and textiles were also important.

Several medium to large-sized towns developed in the area, and spread to form a conurbation stretching almost 100km from west to east.

ocus Point 1

Copy and complete this flow diagram of heavy industry. Fill in the blanks, using these phrases:

- coal mining
- steel making
- heavy engineering
- imported iron ore.

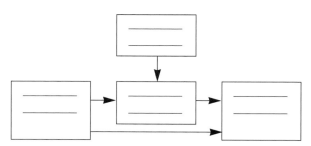

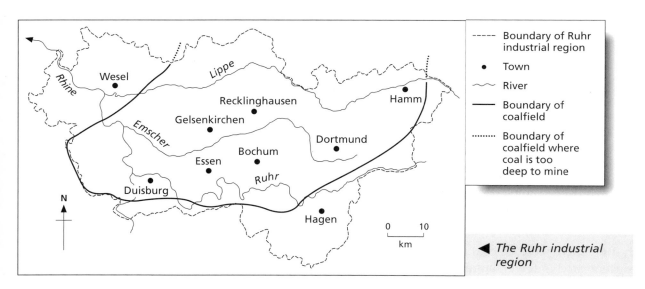

◄ *The Ruhr industrial region*

During the Second World War the Ruhr was one of the main targets for Allied bombers. Much of the industry was damaged. Over 20 per cent of the region's houses were destroyed. However, the area recovered very rapidly as part of the German 'economic miracle'. This was made possible by:

- aid from the USA, which needed West Germany as a strong democratic ally against Communism

- co-operation between the countries of Western Europe, which set up the European Coal and Steel Community (ECSC) to rebuild and modernize these industries across Western Europe as a whole

- the German citizens' hard work and determination.

Coal output reached a peak in 1956. Since then production has declined steadily, as shown by the graphs below.

The steel industry has also declined. It reached peak production later than coal mining and its decline has not been as fast as coal's decline. There has been a big improvement in efficiency because production has been concentrated in two very large, mechanized, integrated steel works.

In 1956 the Ruhr produced 6% of all the world's coal. By 1981 it produced only 2%.

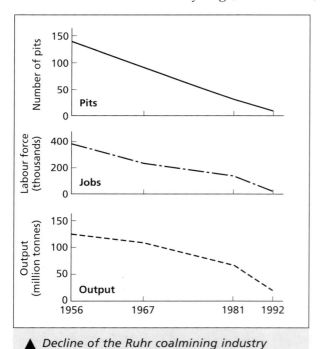

▲ Decline of the Ruhr coalmining industry

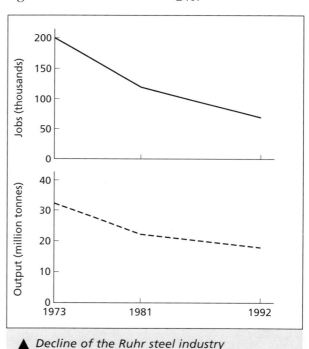

▲ Decline of the Ruhr steel industry

Changing location of the heavy industry

The cross-section on the next page shows how the coal seams come to the surface in the south of the region, along the Ruhr valley. They dip northwards, becoming deeper and more difficult to reach in the Emscher and Lippe valleys. The earliest mines were in the Ruhr valley where the coal was easy to mine, so naturally the coal in this area was exhausted first.

By 1981 there were no coal mines in the Ruhr valley. Work was concentrated in fewer, larger, capital-intensive pits further north. Since

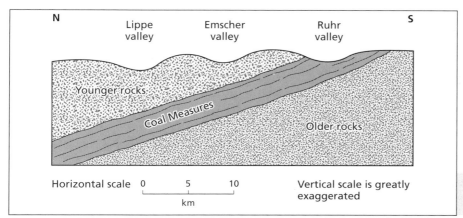

N Lippe S
valley

Emscher
valley

Ruhr
valley

Younger rocks

Coal Measures

Older rocks

Horizontal scale 0 5 10
km

Vertical scale is greatly
exaggerated

◀ *Cross-section through
the Ruhr coalfield*

British miners are
angry that they have
to compete against
subsidized German
coal mines. The UK
mining industry has
declined far faster
than the German
industry because of
this. (See Chapter 3.)

then even the pits in the Emscher valley have closed and all production
is in the far north of the region. Unfortunately the coal here is very
deep and expensive to mine. Although the pits are highly mechanized
and efficient, they all run at a loss and would have to close if the
government did not pay large subsidies.

In 1981 there were seven integrated steel works in the Ruhr region.
These were mainly in the west, close to the Rhine because the iron ore
was brought in by barge along the Rhine. There were also four old,
small steel works in the Ruhr valley, close to their coal supplies.

Now production has been concentrated at two sites:

● at Hamborn, near Duisburg, on the Rhine, and

● at Dortmund, in the heart of the old coal-mining area, on the Emscher.

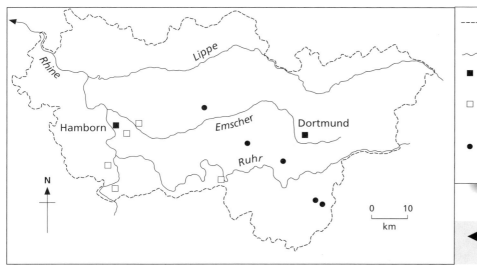

---- Boundary of Ruhr
industrial region

〜 River

■ Integrated steel works
- still open 1998

☐ Integrated steel works
- open in 1983, closed
by 1998

● Other steel works
- open in 1983, closed
by 1998

◀ *Ruhr steel industry,
1983–98*

Managing the changes

Planning in the Ruhr has two main objectives:

1 To improve the environment which had been scarred by mining and
industrial dereliction.

2 To attract new employment to replace jobs lost as heavy industry is
closed down.

Planners have been very successful in achieving the first objective. It has been more difficult to achieve the second, because the area still has a poor image, despite the improvements to the environment.

Reclaiming the environment

The Ruhr has had its own regional planning agency, dealing with environmental problems, since 1920. It is called the Siedlungsverband Ruhrkohlenbezirk (SVR). Its aims are:

- to encourage industrial firms to reduce pollution

- to provide and maintain open space on three different scales:
  - small recreation spaces on the edges of urban areas
  - green wedges preserved between the towns
  - large forested parks surrounding the whole conurbation.

Two particular projects are worth mentioning: the Naturpark Hohe Mark, and the reclamation of the Graf Bismarck pit.

The **Naturpark Hohe Mark** covers about 600 km² on the northern edge of the Ruhr region. It consists mainly of coniferous forest. The SVR's task has been to make this area attractive and accessible to the public. A network of footpaths through the forest has been created, with car parks and cafés for walkers. Water sports facilities have been developed in reservoirs on the edge of the park. It is connected to the urban areas by bus and train services to encourage people to use the facilities.

The **Graf Bismarck Pit** was a large, modern mine near Gelsenkirchen, which was closed in 1966. This left 2 600 000 m² of derelict land and waste tips. These have been remodelled to provide:

- dry ski slopes and other recreational activities

- woodland and nature reserves

- tips for waste disposal in areas of subsidence which have now been filled in and grassed over to produce sports pitches, etc.

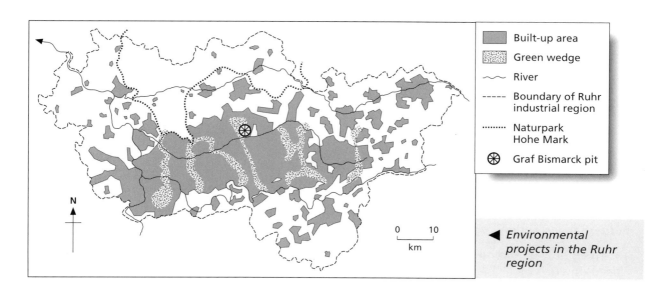

Environmental projects in the Ruhr region

Legend:
- Built-up area
- Green wedge
- River
- Boundary of Ruhr industrial region
- Naturpark Hohe Mark
- Graf Bismarck pit

N

0   10 km

The SVR has been so successful that over 60 per cent of the so-called 'industrial area' of the Ruhr is now classified as green open space.

Attracting new employment

Most modern industry is light and 'footloose'. It is not tied to supplies of energy or raw materials like the old heavy industry was. Managers can choose to locate factories:

- near to the market and to cheap labour supplies
- near to highly-trained labour
- in an area with a good infrastructure of roads, airports, etc.
- in areas that have a good environment, leisure facilities or climate.

Since the 1950s the great growth areas of German industry have been in the south of the country, for example in Bavaria and lower Rhine Valley – Munich, Stuttgart and Frankfurt have been particularly successful in attracting new industries. They have certain advantages over the Ruhr region, because they:

- are warmer, especially in summer
- are near attractive mountains such as the Alps and the Black Forest
- do not have an 'image problem' of being linked with heavy industry.

The new industries in these areas include electronics, automobiles, aircraft, light chemicals (especially drugs), optics (lenses, cameras, telescopes, etc.), and especially IT industries.

In order to try and attract such industries and services the Ruhr planners have had to make many changes. The environmental improvements brought about by the SVR are described above. There have been a number of other changes too.

- New motorways now link the centres of the cities of the conurbation (over 500km of new roads have been built in the area since the 1960s).
- Integrated public transport systems, with buses, trains and city centre tram systems, have been developed. Their timetables are co-ordinated to allow fast, efficient travel within and between towns and cities.
- Three new universities have been opened, in Munster, Marburg and Cologne. They teach science-based courses to produce technicians and engineers, and also provide research facilities for industry.

Despite all these efforts, growth of new employment has been slow.

- Essen, which used to be a main centre of the steel industry, has become a centre for modern office-based work. Many small IT firms have been attracted to the town by the banking and insurance offices that have developed there.
- The government has moved civil service jobs to other towns. It has tried to spread the well-paid office jobs to the towns that need new employment.
- Cologne is the centre of Ford's manufacturing in Germany.

ocus Point 2

What are footloose industries?

Give three reasons why they have mainly been attracted to southern Germany rather than to the Ruhr region.

Hints and Tips!

Learn these five headings for the work done by planners to attract industry:

- motorways
- public transport
- universities
- industrial sites
- environment.

When you know the headings, try to learn two or three details under each one. This will allow you to write elaborated answers in the exam.

Unfortunately, unemployment has remained higher in this region than in the rest of western Germany. Since 1965 there has been a steady trickle of migrants out of the Ruhr region. Most of the people leaving have gone to cities in southern Germany where employment is available, and where the environment is more attractive.

Is the Ruhr region an area of poverty?

Three different answers can be given to this question.

1 Compared with other parts of the EU, like southern Italy, the Ruhr is certainly not an area of poverty. Average wage rates are higher and unemployment is lower than in those areas.

2 Compared with the rest of the old West Germany the Ruhr is quite poor. Unemployment rates are higher than in the south, although people with jobs are still well paid.

3 Compared with most of the old East Germany, the Ruhr is not at all poor. It has a much stronger economy than the east, where many areas still rely on old heavy industry like the Ruhr did in the 1950s.

The Ruhr has been through a great transition in the last 50 years. The changes have been managed very carefully. Some people have suffered, but everything that could be done to smooth out the problems has been done. The Ruhr offers many lessons to other old industrial regions about how to plan for the decline of employment in coal and heavy industries. The area's industries have been modernized, and the environment has been restored with great care.

Hints and Tips!

The three possible answers to this question depend on scale. The scale of an area is always important to geographers, and you should be prepared to think about different scales when you are answering any geography question.

Exam practice

(a) On an outline map of the Ruhr region:

  (i)   mark and name two important towns   (2 marks)

  (ii) write 'early' where coal mining first developed   (1 mark)

  (iii) write 'recent' in the area where mines have been dug most recently   (1 mark)

  (iv) mark and name the location of an integrated steel works operating today. (2 marks)

(b) (i) Give two reasons for the decline in coal production during the last 40 years. (4 marks)

  (ii) Some British miners think the German miners have had an unfair advantage because of their government's policy on the industry. Explain why they think this.   (2 marks)

(c) Choose a project to restore the old industrial landscape of the Ruhr region.

  (i)   Describe the location of the project.   (1 mark)

  (ii) Describe what has been done to restore the environment.   (2 marks)

  (iii) The planners hope that environmental improvements will attract new industry to the area. Why is a good environment important to industry?   (2 marks)

(d) Describe one other project (apart from environmental improvement) to bring industry and jobs back to the Ruhr region.   (3 marks)

11 Tourism in Mediterranean Spain

For this topic you should study:
- location of major tourist areas and reasons for their growth, including a study of the Mediterranean climate
- holiday patterns within Europe (i.e. the origins of tourists to Spain)
- economic importance of tourism
- advantages and disadvantages of tourism to the local economy and environment.

Development of tourism

For many British people Spain **is** the country of holidays. It is associated with 'sun, sea, sand and sangria'. This has come about since the early 1960s due to a combination of factors.

Climate

The two graphs show the temperature and rainfall for Falmouth in south-west Cornwall and Cartagena in south-east Spain. Both places have beautiful scenery, sandy beaches, and many other attractions for holidaymakers, but Spanish resorts have the great advantage of being able to rely on the hot, dry Mediterranean climate in summer.

In summer the area is dominated by high pressure air masses and winds from the east. The air is dry and stable. It brings long periods of cloudless skies, allowing the sun to shine without interruption. This can cause occasional short downpours of convective rain – but these are soon over and rainfall totals are low.

In winter the winds blow in from the Atlantic bringing rainfall, but temperatures stay milder than Britain's, because Spain is further south.

ocus Point 1

Use the graphs to complete the table.

	Cartagena	Falmouth
Average July temperature (°C)		
Average August temperature (°C)		
Average July rainfall total (mm)		
Average August rainfall total (mm)		

What does your table suggest about the number of hours of sunshine and cloud in the two resorts?

What does it suggest about sea temperatures in the two resorts?

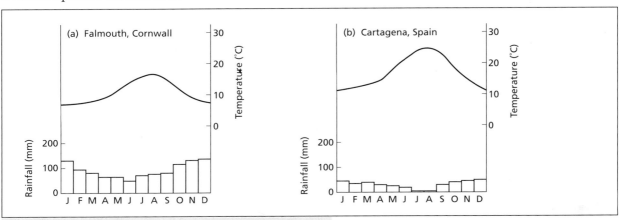

▲ *Climate graphs for (a) Falmouth and (b) Cartagena*

Physical environment

Mainland Spain has over 1000km of coastline on the Mediterranean. In addition the Balearic Islands lie just off the coast. Huge stretches of the coast have sandy beaches, and there are also many attractive, rocky headlands which add to the attraction.

The clear blue skies and clean water combine to make the sea look blue. The low tidal range, the lack of strong currents, and gently sloping sand combine to make the sea safe for bathing in most areas. Just inland there are many areas of attractive scenery which can easily be visited, while on the coast itself there are pretty fishing villages and some beautiful, historic cities and ports like Barcelona and Valencia.

Low wage rates

Average wage rates in Spain have been lower than those in northern Europe throughout the period of the growth of the holiday industry. Since Spain joined the EU in 1986 wages have risen but they are still quite low, so prices in hotels, restaurants, etc. are cheaper than in the UK. This increases Spain's attraction.

Cheap air fares

Mass tourism only really became possible in the 1960s with the development of wide-bodied aircraft, especially the jumbo jet. This meant that people could be moved long distances fairly cheaply. Companies that bought these aircraft had to keep them full and flying by attracting new customers. They created the package-holiday industry, which only makes small profits on each person moved, but attracts huge numbers of people to travel.

Building the resorts

Up until the late 1950s, Spain's tourist industry had been very small. The only foreign tourists who visited the country were 'independent travellers' who had enough time, money and initiative to organize their own travel and to discover interesting little places to stay. These were often small, unspoilt fishing villages, with beautiful beaches that had not been discovered by mass tourism.

Then, over a period of about ten years, the situation changed completely. Businessmen realized what natural advantages the Spanish coast offered – if only facilities could be provided for the mass tourist industry, which would bring people in on cheap flights. This meant investing first in hotels and airports, allowing the area to cater for large numbers. As long as the hotels could be filled they could offer very cheap prices. Once the tourists started coming, the villages became towns, with large hotels, restaurants, clubs, shops, pools and other facilities for tourists.

The boom brought rapid development and improvements in wage rates for many people. The infrastructure of roads, water supply, airports, etc. has also been improved, bringing many benefits to local people.

Development has also caused problems. In many places it has damaged the environment: the scenery has been altered, and often spoilt; water has been polluted; traditional industries such as fishing have been

ocus Point 2

Look back through this section of text.

List five of the Spanish coast's physical attractions for tourists.

DID YOU KNOW?

Companies could only make a profit if they could sell **all** the seats on their planes. This meant that they had to market their holidays with a very heavy programme of advertising. Price cutting, to attract customers from opposing firms, became very common.

Note Remember, jobs in tourism are usually only seasonal. They cannot be relied on to offer a wage all year round.

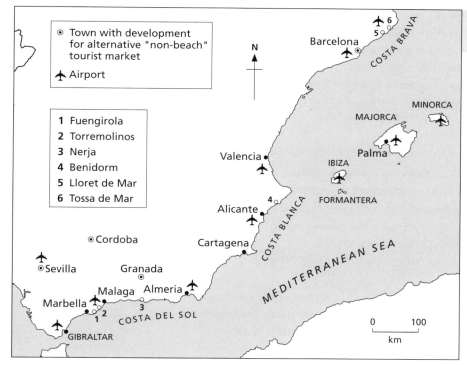

Legend for map:
- ⊙ Town with development for alternative "non-beach" tourist market
- ✈ Airport

1 Fuengirola
2 Torremolinos
3 Nerja
4 Benidorm
5 Lloret de Mar
6 Tossa de Mar

◄ *The Spanish tourist industry*

Majorca shows how resorts specialized in different types of holiday. Resorts around Palma in the south of the island specialized in cheap holidays. Large hotels were built to cater for the 'mass market'. In the north of the island resorts were kept smaller to attract people who wanted a quieter holiday in a more traditional Spanish environment. The smaller numbers of people who came to this area were usually able to pay higher prices than the people staying round Palma.

damaged; and so on. All this has been done to develop tourism, and tourism is a very fickle business. Fashions change, and old resorts can be abandoned when the market for holidays change.

Many tourist resorts go through stages of development, then decline.

• Stage 1 Pioneer development	Single tourists come to explore. There are few facilities. Access is difficult. Local culture is one of the main attractions. The resort becomes fashionable with 'trend-setters'.
• Stage 2 Rapid growth	Facilities are developed. Access becomes easier. Mass tourism starts because of better marketing. Tourism starts to dominate the local economy and culture.
• Stage 3 Saturation stage	There are so many tourists that the area becomes overcrowded. The original attractions of the area start to be spoilt by overuse. Pollution becomes a serious problem and the resort becomes unfashionable. Growth slows down.
• Stage 4 Decline	The market moves on, because the attractions of the area have disappeared. The resort has to seek new gimmicks to attract visitors, or seek new markets.

The following history 'time line' shows how Spain has gone through some of those stages.

1960	Fewer than half a million British visitors.
1971	More than 3 million British visitors.
1988	Over 7.5 million British visitors. Total of 54 million visitors, mainly from northern Europe. Tourism now accounts for 10% of Spain's GNP.

Focus Point 3

Try to work out when the Spanish coastal resorts were in Stages 1, 2 and 3. Do you think they have reached Stage 4 yet?

1989	Total number of visitors fell by 0.2%. Number of British visitors fell by 4%.
1990	Poor exchange rate makes Spain a poor bargain for foreign visitors. Tourist revenue falls by 22.5% 10 000 East Europeans invited to Spain for free holidays in an attempt to open up a new area of the market wanting cheap holidays. Balearic Islands local government invests £65 million in improving infrastructure and environment. Marketing campaign increases number of Japanese visitors by a third.
1990–95	Benidorm invests £317 million in new golf courses, parks and clean-up campaigns to protect environment and attract new visitors.
1990–98	Spanish government invests £50 million in chain of luxury 'Parador' hotels in inland Spain, to attract a new, richer type of tourist. Most of these Paradors are in historic, inland cities. Marketing campaign for 'Green Spain' to attract tourists to new, unspoilt areas.
1996	Plans to build the Costa Doñana resort cancelled partly because of worries over its effect on the environment, and partly because it was seen as unnecessary and would damage other resorts' business.

Hints and Tips!

Learn this brief summary of Mediterranean climate first:

Hot dry summers, warm wet winters.

Then use this chapter's text to fill in some of the details.

The best answers in exams also use some precise statistics, so try to learn some from your table summarizing Cartagena's climate.

Questions

Choose a holiday resort that you have studied.

1   Learn where it is located on the map of Spain.

2   Describe the natural and 'built' attractions of your resort.

3   Describe how the resort has brought advantages and disadvantages to the local people and economy.

4   Describe how the growth of the resort has affected the environment of the area.

Exam practice

(a) Imagine that you are writing an introduction to a travel company's brochure for holidays on the Mediterranean coast of Spain.
  (i)   Write a paragraph to describe the attractions of the climate.   (4 marks)
  (ii) Write another paragraph to describe the scenery and other **natural** attractions of the area for holidaymakers.   (4 marks)

(b) (i)   On an outline map of Spain, mark and name a chosen holiday resort.   (1 mark)
  (ii) Name the region where it is located.   (1 mark)
  (iii) Describe the accommodation and other facilities that have been built for tourists in your chosen resort.   (4 marks)

(c) The growth of the tourist industry has brought both advantages and disadvantages to the local people in the Spanish resorts.
  (i)   Explain one way the local people have benefited from the tourist industry.   (2 marks)
  (ii) Explain one problem that the industry has caused for local people.   (2 marks)

(d) The number of British tourists visiting Spain has fallen in recent years. Describe one way that the industry is trying to deal with the problems caused by this fall.   (2 marks)

12 The Rhine waterway

For this topic you should study:
- the meaning of 'navigable river' and 'head of navigation'
- importance of river traffic and location of the major ports on the Rhine
- types of cargo, their volumes and destinations
- significance of the trade within the economy of the EU.

In the United Kingdom canal transport was very important in the late eighteenth and early nineteenth centuries. It was essential for the early development of the Industrial Revolution. However, once the railway system developed, the canals mostly fell out of use. In continental Europe the inland waterways are still vital for moving many heavy, bulky products like coal, iron ore and grain.

Rivers form the basis of Europe's inland waterway system, but they have often been straightened, and deepened or widened, to take large barges. The main rivers have also been linked by canals, to form a network of interlinked routes. The Rhine is at the centre of this network.

Now, if canals are used at all in the UK, they are almost entirely used for leisure boating.

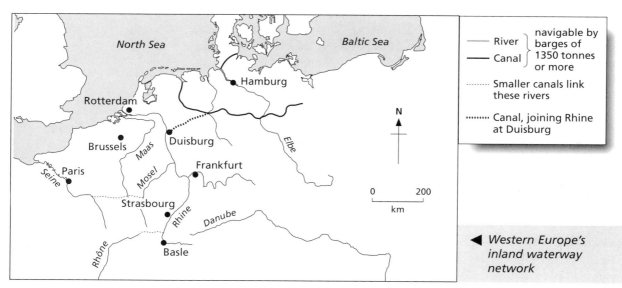

◀ Western Europe's inland waterway network

Water transport is slower than road or rail, but the cost per tonne for each kilometre travelled is lower when the goods are bulky and moved over long distances. As long as they are not perishable, this is an excellent, non-polluting way of moving goods. In fact the governments of Germany and the Netherlands encourage the use of waterways rather than roads for moving freight whenever this is possible. It reduces:

- congestion on the roads
- the use of scarce fossil fuels
- the output of carbon dioxide (which contributes to global warming)
- the output of oxides of sulphur and nitrogen (which cause acid rain).

Hints and Tips!

Learn the phrases **navigable**, **waterway** and **head of navigation**. In the exam you may well be asked what they mean.

The course of the Rhine

The Alpine section

The Rhine rises (starts) in the Alps, in Switzerland. It flows through Lake Constance, and then forms the border between Switzerland and Germany. At Basle it turns to flow northwards and forms the border between France and Germany.

The Rift Valley

Between Basle and Mainz the river flows in a rift valley. The floor of this valley is broad and flat and the river used to meander across the flood plain. The river has been straightened and deepened here. This means that it is **navigable** (barges can travel along it) as far as Basle. Basle is described as the **head of navigation** because barges cannot go any further upstream. Strasbourg lies in this section. It is the main river port in eastern France, and it is linked to the Seine and the Rhône by canals. The Neckar is a tributary which joins the Rhine in this section. It has also been made navigable as far as Stuttgart (in other words, Stuttgart is the head of navigation on the Neckar).

The Rhine Gorge

At Bingen the river enters a steep-sided gorge with a much narrower flood plain. In some places the flood plain disappears completely and the roads and railways alongside the river have to tunnel into the cliffs because there is nowhere else to build them. Navigation here is made difficult by the fast current and the tight bends in the river. There are many rocky cliffs alongside the river in this section. Despite the problems the traffic is very heavy here because more barges join from the Main on the east bank and the Mosel on the west bank.

The Plain section

At Bonn the Rhine leaves the highlands and flows across the North German Plain. Then it crosses the border into the Netherlands, and flows across the delta before reaching the sea through its distributaries, the Lek and the Waal. These have been completely canalized to stop them flooding, and to make them more easily navigable. In this section, traffic on the river is joined by barges from the Ruhr region and from eastern Germany, which have travelled along the Mittelland Canal. Then, in the delta region, the Rhine and the Meuse or Maas navigation systems link together, adding more traffic. The Rhine finally flows to the sea past Rotterdam and Europort.

Traffic on the Rhine

The River Rhine and its tributaries carry four times as much freight as all the other waterways in Europe put together! They form a vital trade link between the North Sea and central Europe. However, this must be kept in proportion. Even in the Rhine valley, road transport is still the most important form of transport.

Strasbourg is one of the homes of the European Union's parliament. It is a symbol of the friendship between France and Germany which has replaced many centuries of war and rivalry in this region.

ocus Point 1

What are the four sections of the Rhine valley called:

(a) to Basle
(b) Basle to Bingen
(c) Bingen to Bonn
(d) below Bonn?

Road 74%	Waterway 22%	Rail 4%

◀ Freight movements in the Netherlands

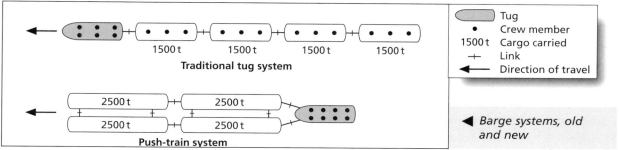

Barge systems, old and new

In the past, tugs were used to pull steel barges loaded with freight. Up to four barges could be pulled in a line, each carrying 1500 tonnes of cargo. Nowadays most of the transport consists of 'push-trains'. In these a very powerful barge, equipped with radar and closed-circuit TV pushes four barges that are linked together in pairs. Each barge can carry between 2000 and 2750 tonnes, and a much smaller crew is needed. The push-trains are also faster than the old tugs.

The type of freight carried has also changed. Forty years ago coal was the most important cargo, sent north and south from the Ruhr coalfield. Iron ore was second most important, transported from the mines in eastern France to the Ruhr region. Production from these mining areas has declined enormously. Now, the main cargoes are:

DID YOU KNOW?

All the locks on the Rhine waterway system are built big enough to take the whole of a push-train without the barges needing to be uncoupled.

North to South (upstream)	South to North (downstream)
Iron ore imported through Rotterdam and taken to the Ruhr region.	**Building materials**, mainly **sand and gravel** deposited by the fast-flowing streams flowing from the Alps.
Scrap metal imported and produced in the Netherlands, and sent to the Ruhr region.	**Manufactured goods** from ports all along the Rhine, sent to Rotterdam for export*.
Oil and oil products imported through Europort and sent to most Rhine ports.	**Coal** still sent from the Ruhr coalfield in small quantities.
Grain and fodder crops imported through Rotterdam and sent to most Rhine ports.	

* Note that many of the manufactured goods are now carried on specialized barges which can carry containers. There are even some specially-built car transporter barges!

The Rhine ports

The table shows the amount of cargo handled by the main Rhine ports.

All these ports have docks built to take barges. In the past, many of the barges were loaded and unloaded using manual labour, but this was slow and became too expensive as the costs of wages rose. Now the docks are highly mechanized.

- Some cargoes can be unloaded by suction, through pipes like giant vacuum cleaners.

- Grain, coal and ore are loaded onto barges automatically. The barge is floated under a conveyor belt, which just pours the cargo in.

- Containers can be lifted on and off by specially-built cranes.

Hints and Tips!

Find all these ports on a map. You should try to learn where they are, so that you can mark them on a map in the exam if necessary. (If you cannot learn them all, try to make sure you know Rotterdam, Duisburg, Strasbourg and Basle.)

At these ports cargo is transferred from river to land transport, so railways and roads link up with the river here. There are large areas for storage of cargo awaiting transfer to the next form of transport.

		Cargo handled (million tonnes/yr)
Rotterdam	Netherlands	233.4*
Duisburg-Ruhrort	Germany	20.5
Cologne	Germany	12.0
Strasbourg	France	11.7
Frankfurt (on Main)	Germany	10.2
Mannheim	Germany	8.6
Basle	Switzerland	8.0

* Includes ocean traffic as well as inland waterway traffic.

Industry is attracted to the ports too, especially industry that processes raw materials. The point where cargoes are loaded and unloaded is sometimes called a **break-of-bulk** point. Transport costs can be saved if materials can be processed at the break-of-bulk point, rather than having to make another journey to the factory. An extra journey would involve extra costs, so there are big savings to be made by locating industry close to the port.

ocus Point 2

Cover up this table. Name three types of goods that are carried from north to south, and three that are carried from south to north.

Then add at least one elaboration to each item in your list. Remember that you need these elaborations if you are to gain high-level marks in the exam.

Hints and Tips!

You may have noticed that some of these methods are very similar to those used in modern English ports (see Chapter 7). It may be easier to learn this if you remember the similarities.

Exam practice

(a) (i)   Which mountain range is the source of the Rhine?   (1 mark)

(ii) Name four countries that the Rhine flows through, or for which the river is a border.   (2 marks)

(iii) Name two tributaries of the Rhine.   (1 mark)

(iv) What name is given to the section of the Rhine between Basle and Bingen?   (1 mark)

(v) Name the port at the mouth of the Rhine.   (1 mark)

(b) (i)   The Rhine is a navigable river. What does 'navigable' mean?   (1 mark)

(ii) Basle is the head of navigation of the Rhine. What does 'head of navigation' mean?   (1 mark)

(iii) Much of the freight traffic on the Rhine is carried by 'push-trains' of barges. Explain why these are more efficient than the old system of tugs and barges.   (3 marks)

(c) (i)   Describe the main types of cargo carried along the Rhine:
   • from north to south
   • from south to north.   (4 marks)

(ii) Suggest why the cargoes carried southwards are different from those carried northwards.   (2 marks)

(d) Choose a port on the Rhine (apart from Rotterdam).

(i)   Mark and name it on an outline map of the Rhine valley.   (1 mark)

(ii) Describe the industry that has developed in and around that port.   (2 marks)

13 The growth of Rotterdam/Europort

For this topic you should study:
- the location of Rotterdam/Europort
- the reasons for the growth of the port and the idea of a hinterland
- links with the hinterland by ship, barge, road, rail and pipeline
- port facilities and functions, containerization and oil terminals.

Development of Rotterdam up to 1945

Rotterdam was originally built 16km from the sea on the little River Rotte which was one of the distributaries of the Rhine. Rotterdam was sited where a dam was built across the Rotte to stop sea water flooding inland during storms. A port grew at this point, because boats from the sea could not travel farther inland.

Rotterdam's main growth began in 1870. There were three main reasons for this.

- A treaty was signed to allow all states along the Rhine to trade their goods on the river. This led to much more trade passing to the North Sea through Rotterdam.

- In 1872 the New Waterway was built. This is a major canal that allowed very large ocean-going ships to reach Rotterdam.

- The Ruhr valley was industrializing very rapidly, and Rotterdam handled the Ruhr's trade with the rest of the world.

By the 1930s Rotterdam had become one of the most important ports in the world. Its docks and industry had started to spread westwards, along the New Waterway towards the North Sea. However, the Second World War destroyed large areas of industry, docks and housing, so by the end of 1945 the city needed massive rebuilding.

The new ports built since 1945

Before the war the port was being extended westwards. After the war this new building speeded up.

- **Eemhaven** was completed in 1967. Three dock basins were built into the land alongside the New Waterway. This was then the biggest container terminal in the world. It was built with special cranes for loading, unloading, storing and sorting containers.

- **Botlek** was built in 1957, mainly as a port for oil imports. Industry has developed around the oil terminals here and in Europort.

- **Europort** was built during the 1960s and 70s. A whole series of docks were excavated on the island of Rozenburg. (The earth that was dug out was used to raise the level of the island to 5 metres above sea-level

Obviously Rotterdam was named after the 'dam' on the 'Rotte'. Amsterdam has a similar site, which also gave the city its name – after the 'dam' on the 'Amstel'.

Hints and Tips!

You cannot understand Rotterdam properly unless you also know about the Rhine waterway and the Ruhr industrial region. Try to revise these three chapters (10, 12 and 13) together, and look for cross-references.

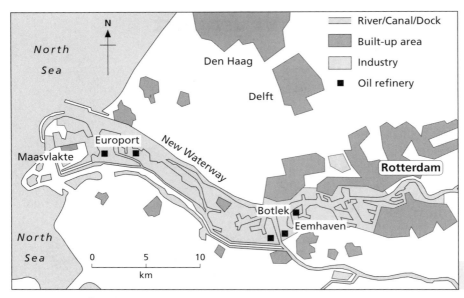

◀ *Rotterdam/Europort*

to stop it flooding.) This has more oil tanker terminals and also handles bulk carriers with cargoes of iron ore, other ores, coal and grain.

- **Maasvlakte** is built on land reclaimed from the North Sea (completed in 1974). It has become a port for handling bulk carriers and has a bigger container terminal than Eemhaven. Land is reserved for port facilities. Little industry has developed.

The growth of the oil and petrochemicals industries

Huge supertankers bring crude oil into the docks at Maasvlakte and Europort. Specialized equipment unloads the oil as quickly so that the tanker does not waste time in port. The crude oil is stored in huge, cylindrical storage tanks, grouped together near the terminal in 'tank farms'.

Most of the crude oil is then sent to one of the five major oil refineries built close to the port. Here the crude oil is broken down into a number of separate substances, by 'cracking'. This is done by heating the crude

Rotterdam is the biggest oil port in Europe. Many traders meet at the Rotterdam oil market to buy and sell oil. The price everyone in Britain pays for their petrol is largely decided here, and depends on the amount the traders pay to buy their crude oil.

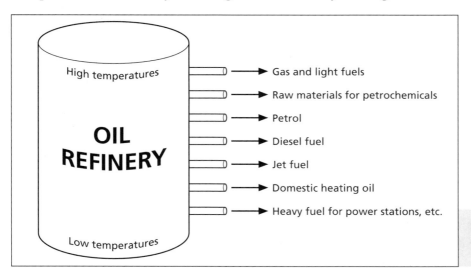

◀ *Some of the products of an oil refinery cracking tower*

oil until it vaporizes. The gases rise up inside a tall, cylindrical structure called a 'cracking tower'. The less dense substances rise to the top of the tower, but the denser substances stay near the base. The different substances (or 'fractions') can be piped out of the tower at each level.

Some of the products can be used straight away, but others have to be processed further. They are used as the basis for a whole new industry – petrochemicals. The elements in the oil fractions have to be taken apart and put back together again in different combinations in a petrochemical plant. The products made include fertilizers; pesticides; plastics; rubber; paint; dyes; disinfectants; food additives; drugs; etc.

Petrochemical plants consist of complex networks of pipelines, pressurized containers, heating systems, cooling towers, and so on. They are like huge, complicated, magnified versions of some of the experiments that you use in chemistry lessons. They are very capital intensive – which means that a lot of money has to be spent setting up the plant. They are often controlled by computer systems and need only a small workforce of very skilled engineers and technicians.

Distribution of goods to Rotterdam's hinterland

By barge
Most of the bulky goods for distribution to the hinterland are carried along the inland waterways by barge. The organization of barge transport is described on page 85 in Chapter 12. The Rhine river system allows goods to reach all of the Netherlands, western Germany, Luxembourg, eastern France and northern Switzerland.

This barge system does not just extend along the Rhine. The river system is linked by a series of canals to other parts of Europe. The Mittelland Canal is probably the most important of these as far as Rotterdam is concerned. It allows the port's hinterland to be extended throughout the northern part of Germany. Rotterdam can compete with ports like Hamburg and Emden for the trade from this region.

The canal that links the Rhine Waterway to the Danube allows Rotterdam to extend its hinterland to southern Germany and Austria.

By rail
The movement of freight by rail has declined enormously over the last 50 years. However, it is still used to move large, heavy loads. The rail network is more extensive than the waterway network, so it carries goods to areas that cannot easily be reached by barge.

It is also faster than barge transport. There are railway lines running along both sides of the Rhine valley, and trains are sometimes used in preference to the barges when speed is important.

By road
The vast majority of Rotterdam's trade in goods other than bulky raw materials, is carried by road. Most manufactured goods brought to Rotterdam either as imports or exports are carried by road on the overland leg of their journey. Since the integration of European Union

In the petrochemical industry the waste products of one plant become the raw materials of the next plant. Petrochemical plants are linked to each other by systems of pipelines. This means that once one chemical works has been set up, it often attracts many others to the same location. This certainly happened around Europort.

'Hinterland' is a German word. Literally it means 'the land behind'. It is used to refer to the area inland from a port that exports and imports goods through that port.

Focus Point 1

What are push-trains? If you are not sure, look back to page 85.

economies, the hinterland of Rotterdam has expanded even more. Routes from all of central Europe are linked to Rotterdam. Lorries can move goods to Rotterdam very quickly, and then its position at the southern end of the North Sea allows easy access to the Atlantic.

Rotterdam's hinterland, its trade and its wealth have grown because of:

- its position
- the integration of Europe's economy through the EU
- its excellent road links
- its very modern, efficient port facilities.

All countries have their own system of road numbering. In the UK motorways are classified as M and the main roads are all A or B roads. The main routes that cross European borders are now classified as E roads.

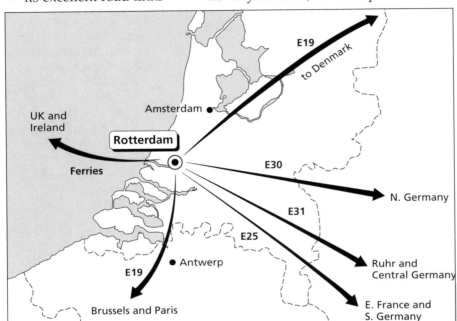

◀ *Rotterdam: Euroroute road focus*

Exam practice

(a) (i) Name the canal that was built in 1872 to link the Rhine to the North Sea, which passed through Rotterdam. (1 mark)

   (ii) Name two of the port areas that have been built on the south side of this canal in the area between Rotterdam and the sea. (2 marks)

(b) (i) What does the word 'hinterland' mean? (2 marks)

   (ii) Name four countries that lie in the hinterland of Rotterdam's port. (2 marks)

   (iii) Name one canal that links to the Rhine and helps to increase the area of Rotterdam's hinterland. (1 mark)

(c) (i) How has the growth of the European Union (EU) helped the growth of the port of Rotterdam? (2 marks)

   (ii) Rotterdam has become a focus for 'E roads'. Explain how this has helped the growth of the port. (2 marks)

(d) 'Containerization' has helped Rotterdam to become more efficient and profitable.

   (i) Explain what 'containerization' means. (2 marks)

   (ii) How has it made the port more efficient and profitable? (2 marks)

(e) Why has the chemical industry become Rotterdam's most important manufacturing industry? (4 marks)

The Wider World

14 Amazonia

For this topic you should study:

- the equatorial forest environment, with particular reference to:
  - description and simple explanation of the annual distribution of temperature and rainfall, including the causes of convective rainfall
  - relationships between climate, soil and vegetation in the ecosystem
  - traditional subsistence and modern farming systems
- communications, with particular reference to:
  - why the Amazon was the earliest transport route
  - route of the Trans-Amazonian Highway
  - expansion of the road network, its impact on the natural environment and traditional activities, and its role in the integration of Amazonia with the rest of Brazil

Most of Amazonia consists of the low, flat flood plain drained by the Amazon River and its tributaries. Large parts of the Andes range drain into the Amazon from the west. The older and lower Venezuelan highlands to the north and the Brazilian highlands to the south are also drained by tributaries. The Amazon is the world's second longest river, after the Nile. However, very high rainfall in many parts of the huge basin means that the Amazon has a much bigger volume of water than the Nile.

The Amazon basin contains the largest rainforest on Earth, and large parts of Amazonia are still not fully explored. Much of the forest is still

◀ *Amazonia*

So much water flows into the Atlantic from the mouth of the Amazon that the water is still fresh enough to drink about 90km from the coast.

largely unaffected by human activity, but development now threatens many areas of forest. To understand how the rainforest works, and how it can be damaged, it is useful to see the forest as a system, with inputs, processes and outputs.

The tropical rainforest environment – a system model

Inputs → | Processes / Flows / Stores | → Outputs

The main **inputs** are:

- minerals from soil

- heat + light from the sun (temperature is high all year)

- moisture from rainfall (rain falls all year round)

Plants can grow for 12 months every year.

The main **storages** in the system are:

in the soil	• minerals from weathered rock
	• **humus** from decayed plant and animal material
	• water
in the vegetation	• minerals and nutrients are used to form plant matter (**biomass**)
on the ground	• dead and decaying plant matter (**litter**)

In the rainforest ecosystem more energy and nutrients are stored in the vegetation than in the soil. This is because the decay of dead matter, and the take-up of nutrients by the plants, is so fast in the hot, humid environment.

Flows constantly transfer matter and energy from soil to vegetation to the litter layer and back into the soil. These flows include:

- the take-up of water and minerals by the plant roots

- dead leaves falling to the ground

- decayed leaf material being carried into the soil by worms.

When rainforest is left in its natural state there are very few **outputs**.

- Water is lost from leaf surfaces by **evapotranspiration**.

- Some water runs into rivers as **throughflow** or **overland flow**.

- Water running through the soil **leaches** some minerals out of the soil.

The main thing that limits growth of new plants is shortage of sunlight. The thick canopy cuts out about 80% of sunlight and makes the forest floor a very shady place.

Rainforests have very luxuriant vegetation but soils are usually very poor. This is because most of the nutrients are taken up by fast-growing plants.

Focus Point 1

Cover up the page. Explain why rainforest trees often have tall, straight trunks and a thick canopy of leaves.

Some important **processes**:

- Photosynthesis

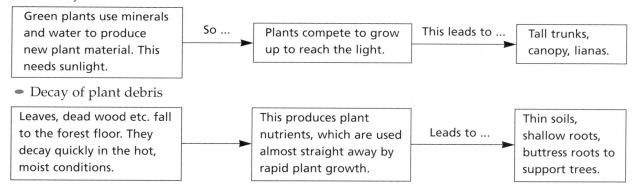

| Green plants use minerals and water to produce new plant material. This needs sunlight. | So ... → | Plants compete to grow up to reach the light. | This leads to ... → | Tall trunks, canopy, lianas. |

- Decay of plant debris

| Leaves, dead wood etc. fall to the forest floor. They decay quickly in the hot, moist conditions. | → | This produces plant nutrients, which are used almost straight away by rapid plant growth. | Leads to ... → | Thin soils, shallow roots, buttress roots to support trees. |

When human activity alters the natural ecosystem, changes to the outputs can take place. For instance:

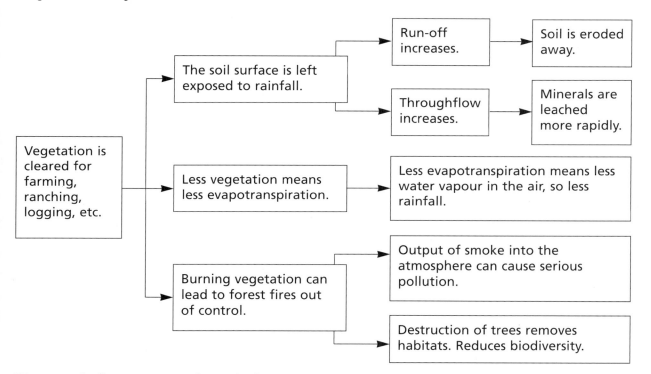

Vegetation is cleared for farming, ranching, logging, etc.

The soil surface is left exposed to rainfall.
→ Run-off increases. → Soil is eroded away.
→ Throughflow increases. → Minerals are leached more rapidly.

Less vegetation means less evapotranspiration. → Less evapotranspiration means less water vapour in the air, so less rainfall.

Burning vegetation can lead to forest fires out of control.
→ Output of smoke into the atmosphere can cause serious pollution.
→ Destruction of trees removes habitats. Reduces biodiversity.

Human influences on the rainforest ecosystem

People have always made use of rainforests. They have used the land for farming and mining, they have used the trees for fruit, nuts, medicines, building wood, firewood and even for magic rituals, and they have hunted and domesticated animals and birds. However, in the past forty years or so the rate of use has increased, and the area that is seriously affected has grown rapidly.

Many human activities can be sustainable, if they are well managed; but if they are badly managed they can destroy the ecosystem on which they are based. Some examples are given on page 94.

Sustainable development means:

- encouraging development so that people can have an improved standard of living

- making sure that the environment is not destroyed, so that the improved standard of living will last.

	More sustainable	Less sustainable
Shifting cultivation	small groups of people use the land to grow crops. Patches of forest are cleared; crops are grown; soil fertility declines; the patch is abandoned and left to recover. The group move on to a new patch of land.	The population of tribes has grown as health care has been improved. Other groups have lost some of their traditional land to outsiders. In both cases they have to use land more intensively. This takes more out of the soil, so it has less time to recover.
Timber	Trees have always been cut by local people to use for building and fuelwood. They took what they needed and left the rest of the forest unchanged. Some commercial timber companies (e.g. in Thailand) replant trees in areas they clear. They plant species that will be useful later. This reduces biodiversity, but does maintain forest cover.	Logging companies use large machines to cut roads through the forest, and then to cut the trees they need. They often clear unwanted trees to allow access to the few valuable trees. Unwanted trees and plants are burnt. This leads to whole areas being cleared of vegetation.
Commercial farming	Plantations for rubber in Malaysia and palms in West Africa have been developed to conserve the soil by making sure that there is always some plant cover to reduce the rate of leaching. They also employ local labour, providing training and good working conditions.	In Amazonia large firms clear enormous areas for cattle ranching. Natural vegetation is burnt; grass is planted; cattle graze the area for a few years; then the soil is exhausted and the land is abandoned. The forest does not re-grow as such large areas have been cleared so that seeds can only spread back very slowly. Soil is often very badly eroded.
Mining	Mining can never be truly sustainable. It uses up resources. But in the Carajas region of Brazil the mining company aims to mine iron ore without damaging the forest around the mine. The whole mine area is strictly controlled to stop squatter settlements developing around the mine and the town where workers live.	In Amazonia, mining of iron ore, gold, etc. has caused great damage. Natives have been killed or removed; forest has been totally destroyed, for the mines and for towns, roads and railways. Then large numbers of squatters have moved into the area to make money growing food for the miners, or seeking casual work at the mines. They cause deforestation to spread out from the original mining area.

Farming and its impact on the environment

Deforestation can bring many important changes to the environment. Many of them are damaging, although it is difficult to get precise information about the effects. The effects can be seen at the local, regional and even global scale. Some of them are described below.

Local-scale effects

1 **Soil erosion** – loss of vegetation removes protection for the soil. Leaves intercept rainfall, and roots bind the soil together. When trees are gone, the soil can be washed away easily.

2 **Soil degradation** – low nutrient content of the soil means that when the vegetation is removed, the soil soon loses its fertility. Nutrients are washed out of the soil (leached) and the soil becomes useless.

3 **Sediment in rivers** – is increased, because of the soil erosion. When it is deposited it can block rivers and cause flooding.

Regional-scale effects

1 **Loss of biodiversity** – the rainforest contains many species that are useful, and many more that may be useful in future. Clearing the forest can lead to extinction of both plant and animal species.

2 **Loss of native peoples** – as the environment is altered, some tribes have been wiped out. Others have lost their culture and become absorbed into Brazilian society. New diseases have also been introduced which have caused great suffering to the tribal people.

3 **Change in the water cycle** – some estimates suggest that 50 per cent of all the rain falling on a rainforest is evaporated from the ground and then forms cloud and rain. If the forest is cleared, the rate of run-off increases. This means that less water is evaporated, so rainfall totals over the whole region are reduced.

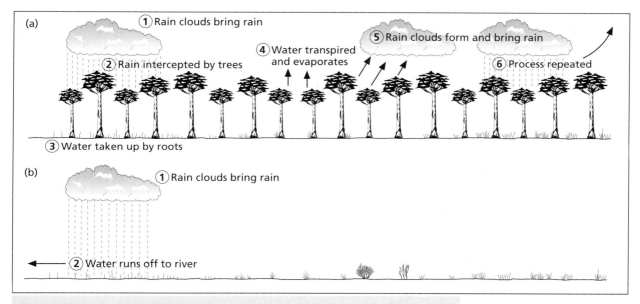

▲ *Rainfall and the rainforest*
(a) Water recycled by the rainforest　(b) Water cycle after deforestation

Global effects

Changes to carbon dioxide in the atmosphere – trees contain carbon taken from the air during photosynthesis. When a tree is burnt, the carbon is released into the atmosphere as carbon dioxide. This adds to the greenhouse effect, increasing global warming.

Burning of the rainforest is a less important cause of global warming than the burning of fossil fuels. Some scientists even say it is not a cause of the greenhouse effect, because new plant growth which replaces burnt forest uses up the carbon that was released by the burning.

However, conserving the rainforest is important for many reasons, and citizens of more developed countries should help the Brazilians to develop their economy without causing further enormous losses of rainforest.

Focus Point 2

Cover up the page. List the effects of deforestation, including:

two local-scale effects

two regional-scale effects

one global effect.

The climate of Amazonia

Temperature

The graph shows high temperatures at all seasons. This is due to the position of the overhead sun. In March and September the sun is directly overhead at the Equator, so its rays are concentrated when they reach the surface in Amazonia. This causes the high temperatures.

In June the sun is overhead at the Tropic of Cancer, and in December it is overhead at the Tropic of Capricorn. Its rays are still fairly concentrated over Amazonia, so temperatures remain high. The south of the region has a slight maximum in December/January and the north has its maximum in June/July.

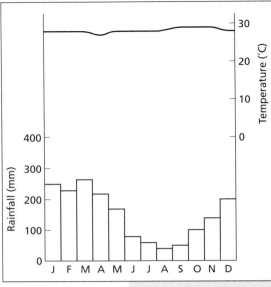

▲ Climate of Manaus

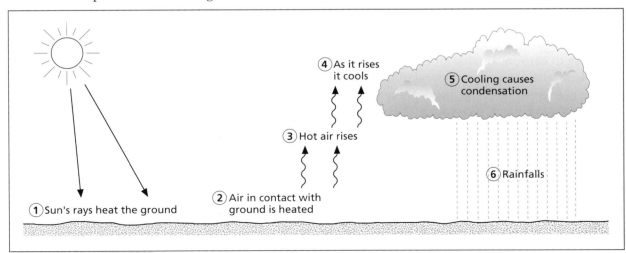

March and September

Sun overhead at equator. Rays concentrated.

Near the poles the rays are more spread out.

June and December

Sun's rays are still fairly concentrated at the equator, although the sun is actually overhead at the tropic.

Focus Point 3

Use the graph to describe the temperature and rainfall distribution in Amazonia. Then read the text to check that you have covered the main

◀ Effects of the sun's rays at the Equator

Rainfall

The high temperatures result in high rainfall. The causes of convective rainfall are explained on the diagram below.

① Sun's rays heat the ground
② Air in contact with ground is heated
③ Hot air rises
④ As it rises it cools
⑤ Cooling causes condensation
⑥ Rainfalls

▲ Convective rainfall

Because the temperature is high throughout the year, rainfall is heavy in all seasons too. In fact rain falls on 300 days a year or more, in many parts of Amazonia. It has been said that there is more variation in the weather on a single day than there is between the seasons.

Communications in Amazonia

Good transport is essential for economic development. Without it, trade is almost impossible. Amazonia has conditions which make transport very difficult. The area's problems include:

- dense, impenetrable rainforest still covers vast areas

- the low, flat land and heavy rainfall cause large areas to flood

- many large rivers form barriers to land transport

- heavy rain causes landslides and erosion that may wash roads away

- large distances and sparse population mean that it is often uneconomic to build transport infrastructure.

When Amazonia was first explored by European settlers, their main routeways were the rivers themselves. The Amazon and its main tributaries are very wide and deep. Ocean-going boats can penetrate as far inland as Manaus, 1500km from the sea. Almost all Amazonia's other towns are also sited on navigable rivers.

As the area was opened up to trade in the nineteenth and twentieth centuries, the economy went through a series of booms and busts. First explorers collected Brazil nuts for export; then rubber was collected from trees growing wild in the forest; then rubber trees were cultivated; timber was exploited; and so on. Each new development relied on river transport to bring in supplies and to export the products.

From the 1930s air transport largely took over from river transport. River transport was too slow and unreliable. Only a few ports could be served on a regular basis; floods and low water made services unpredictable and docks difficult to maintain; and the small volume of traffic meant that services struggled to make a profit.

Small aircraft companies could provide a quick service for freight and passengers, and they could respond in a very flexible way to demands for service. All they needed was a small landing strip, which was cheaper and easier to maintain than the docks in the river ports.

The Trans-Amazonian Highway

In the 1960s the Brazilian government decided that it was essential for the country to 'open Amazonia up for development' because:

- Development was very unevenly spread. Large parts of Amazonia were completely unused.

- There were many poor, landless peasants, especially in the north-east, who needed their own land.

Hints and Tips!

In the exam you may be asked a question about the conflict between conservation and development. Try to give both sides of the argument in a balanced way. In conclusion you can give your own opinions, but support them with facts and figures.

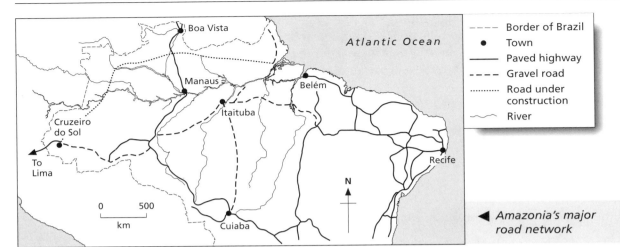

Amazonia's major road network

- Amazonia has huge resources of wood, minerals, HEP potential, etc. These cannot be developed without good access.

- If places on the edges of Amazonia remained unsettled they could be occupied and claimed by neighbouring countries. Brazil could not defend them unless they were more accessible.

A network of roads was planned and built. The main road, the Trans-Amazonian Highway, was opened in 1975. It runs for 5500km from Recife to the Peruvian border. The network is still being developed in the late 1990s. As well as building the road the government has taken other steps to encourage development.

- Land near the road is reserved for settlement and development. Some is sold to large corporations; some is given to poor farmers.

- A commercial centre, with shops and markets, has been set up, about every 100km along the road.

- 'Growth poles' for development have been established. These include mines (for iron ore, bauxite, tin and gold), HEP schemes, commercial farming and forestry.

The highways and the environment

The development of Amazonia, made possible by the new highways, has caused much concern about the environment. Despite the problems, the Brazilian government feels that it is essential to press ahead with development. The country's social problems are so serious that something has to be done to help the poor. This is one of the cheapest ways of giving opportunities to some of those people.

The new settlers cannot concern themselves with long-term conservation – they worry about survival. They exploit their new land, and when the ground loses its fertility they move on and clear more land. Every time this happens, the problems of soil erosion, loss of habitat and loss of species, are increased.

Focus Point 5

This map may seem to show a very well-developed network of routes. Note the scale, though. If you measure some of the distances between roads you will realize just how basic the network still is.

Perhaps concentrating development at the growth poles will help to conserve other areas of the rainforest. It may be useful to think of the growth poles as 'honeypots' for development. (See the Chapter 6, page 00.)

Anyone who is concerned about the problems of deforestation must also consider the problems of Brazil's poor. If they are to be stopped from exploiting the rainforest resources, an alternative must be found. Can an alternative, sustainable development policy stop the damage to Amazonia?

Hints and Tips!

In your examination you may not be able to provide easy answers to this question of an alternative, sustainable development policy, but you must be aware of the issues, and you must be able to consider the point of view of Brazil's landless poor!

Exam practice

(a) In the UK the average monthly temperature is about 17°C in July and about 4°C in January. The seasonal pattern of temperature in Amazonia is very different from this.

   (i)   Describe the seasonal pattern of temperature in Amazonia.   (2 marks)

   (ii) Explain why Amazonia has very high temperatures.   (3 marks)

(b) Many parts of Amazonia have over 2000mm of rainfall per year. Rain falls on more than half the days in the year. Explain what causes this rainfall. You may use a diagram to help your explanation.   (4 marks)

(c) (i)   In the rainforest vegetation system, what is:
   • the canopy
   • an emergent
   • a buttress root?   (3 marks)

   (ii) Choose one of the vegetation features listed in (i). Explain how the climate and soil conditions cause it to develop.   (3 marks)

(d) (i)   Give one reason why the Brazilian government decided to build the Trans-Amazonian Highway.   (1 mark)

   (ii) How has the construction of this highway damaged the rainforest ecosystem?   (4 marks)

(e) Clearing rainforest causes (i) exposed soil, (ii) reduced evapotranspiration, and (iii) forest fires. Describe how each of these can cause problems for people and the environment.   (3 marks)

15 A The formation and features of the Ganges delta

For this topic you should study:
- subsistence rice farming in a hazardous physical environment, with particular reference to:
  - the location of the Ganges delta, its formation and physical features
  - advantages and disadvantages of this region for settlement and farming
  - causes of flooding
  - description of tropical monsoon climate
  - effects of monsoon failure and tropical storms
  - effects of the introduction of intermediate technology and scientific developments
  - foreign aid, its implications and issues; successes and failures of development.

The map below shows the drainage basin of the Ganges river system. To the north lie the Himalayas and to the south is the Deccan Plateau. The river flows into the Bay of Bengal, through its **delta**. Here the river splits up into smaller channels, called **distributaries**.

The Himalayas are recent fold mountains. Many fast-flowing streams carry eroded sediment down from the mountains, and much of this has been deposited to form the flood plain of the Ganges basin.

- This sediment, which is renewed every year by flood water, provides excellent soils for rice cultivation.

- The area's monsoon climate provides ideal rainfall and temperature conditions for rice growing.

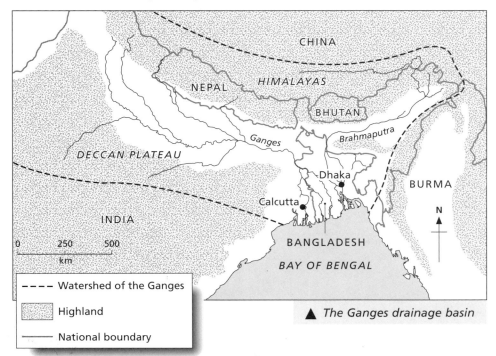

▲ *The Ganges drainage basin*

The tropical monsoon climate

The Ganges basin lies in the region of monsoon climate. This means that the seasonal pattern of rainfall is very uneven.

There are three main seasons in the Ganges basin (see graph).

1 **The hot dry season**   The sun is overhead in the northern hemisphere. The interior of northern India is heated intensely. A low pressure air system develops over northern India.

2 **The wet season**   Air is drawn in towards the area of low pressure. The air comes off the sea, and because it is hot it carries lots of water vapour. When the air is forced to rise over the coast (and even more over the Himalayan foothills), it brings very heavy rainfall.

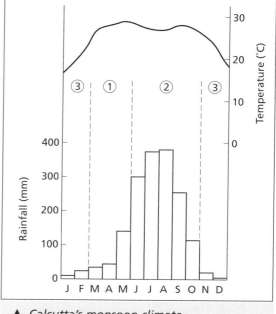

▲ *Calcutta's monsoon climate*

3 **The cool dry season**   The sun is overhead in the southern hemisphere. Air over northern India becomes cooler. This forms a high pressure air system. Cool winds blow out from the area of high pressure. The winds are dry because they form over land.

The farmers in the area rely heavily on this pattern of rainfall. Their agricultural calendar is built around the rain, the floods, and irrigation water brought by the rivers. If the rains are early the preparation of the fields may not be complete, causing problems for the farmers.

The problems are worse when the rains are late, or when less rain falls than expected. Then the season can be cut short and yields can be lower than needed. When yields fall, subsistence farmers may have to take out loans, at high interest, so that they can buy food to survive. Shortages drive up the price of rice, causing even greater problems for subsistence farmers and for the poor in the towns.

Hints and Tips!

Do not think of India's climate in terms of spring, summer, autumn and winter. These terms will only confuse you. Use the names of the three seasons given in the text.

Flooding in the Ganges basin – physical factors

Rainfall is concentrated in the period between April and September, and so the rivers regularly flood after the period of heavy rainfall. Farmers rely on the floods to provide water for the crops and sediment to fertilize the fields. In the dry season, rivers fall to low levels.

Cyclones

Cyclones can also cause flooding at certain times of the year.

- A lot of the precipitation in the Himalayas falls as snow. This builds up during the winter, then melts during the thaw. Meltwater can cause floods downstream.

- Between August and October, tropical cyclones form over the Bay of Bengal. They blow in towards the coast of Bangladesh and north-east India. They bring heavy rain and tidal surges, which both increase the flood risk in the lower valley and the delta.

The effects of cyclones

Two of the most disastrous cyclones to hit the Ganges delta struck in 1970 and 1985. In 1970 a storm surge wave over 8m high flooded the delta. 300 000 people died, and 1 million were left homeless.

An even bigger wave struck in 1985. Estimated at 9m in height, it flooded 150km inland across the flat delta. Only 40 000 people lost their lives this time, but an enormous relief effort had to be mounted.

- In the **short term** it was important to try to rescue as many of the people stranded by the waves as possible. This was difficult because almost all the area's roads and railways had been cut. Helicopters and boats were the only ways of reaching the survivors.

- In the **medium term** it was vital to prevent an outbreak of typhoid. The flood had contaminated water supplies with sewage and dead bodies. Disease could have spread very rapidly if it once became established.

- In the **long term** the people had to be fed. The flood had destroyed the rice crop and contaminated the soil with salt water. People needed emergency food supplies, but they also needed help to reclaim their land, replace lost cattle and rebuild their ruined fishing boats.

Managing the effects of cyclones

Cyclones contain absolutely enormous amounts of energy. It is impossible for people to control such powerful forces, but careful management can reduce their damaging effects by:

- long-term planning in areas where storms are common

- studying and tracking storms once they form

- action as the storm approaches, to minimize damage.

Planning for cyclones in Bangladesh

The Flood Action Plan (FAP) is an attempt by the Bangladeshi authorities and international aid donors to tackle the area's problems. Projects that are being researched, and which may be built over the next 30 years, include:

- improved satellite weather forecasting, to allow better prediction

- reinforcing coastal banks to protect land and people from floods

- raising the mounds that people live on, so that they are above the level of the highest floods

- improving roads so that aid can be delivered more easily

- building concrete storm shelters.

DID YOU KNOW?

When the monsoon causes the Ganges to flood, the water usually rises slowly and predictably. People can prepare for the flood. Tropical storms are usually sudden and far less predictable. Therefore the floods they bring can cause far more damage.

Focus Point 1

List four aspects of the human and physical geography of Bangladesh that make tropical storms here particularly dangerous.

List four ways of reducing the damage done by cyclones in Bangladesh's Flood Action Plan.

Flooding in the Ganges basin – human factors

In this section it is important to ask three questions about the interrelationship between the rivers and the people.

1 Are human activities increasing flooding?

In many parts of the catchment area of the Ganges, deforestation is taking place. People clear trees for farmland, and to provide fuelwood and building material. It seems certain that this has led to increased flooding in parts of Nepal and Bhutan, close to where the clearance has taken place. This is a result of:

- less **interception** of rainfall by plant leaves

- less **infiltration** of water into the soil, because land that is not protected by vegetation gets baked hard by the sun

- less **take-up** of water by plant roots

- more **erosion** of soil, because it is no longer bound together by plant roots. This leads to deposition of sediment on the flood plains, blocking rivers.

On the other hand, there has been an increase in the number of cyclones coming from the Bay of Bengal. They have also caused greater damage and loss of life, because population growth means more people are now forced to live on the flood plains. The floods cause more death and damage, even though they are no higher than in the past.

2 How important are the floods to people who live near to the rivers?

The regular, annual flooding is vital to the people who live on the flood plain of the Ganges. People have adapted their lives to the floods. Most people live on mounds of land, above the normal flood level. The roads and tracks are also built along natural or artificial banks.

The farming season is planned around the floods. Rice is the main crop and there are many different varieties. Each is adapted to slight differences in temperature, length of growing season, and depth of the flood water in the fields. The various types are planted in different areas as the flood waters advance and then retreat. Without the floods the very high population densities in this area could not be supported by the land.

Seasonally flooded land also provides feeding grounds for fish. They provide a vital food source for the inhabitants. For many poor people, fish from their fields are their main source of protein.

3 What is being done, and what more could be done, to reduce the damaging effects of the floods?

After the 1988 floods the Bangladesh government and international aid donors set up the **Flood Action Plan** (FAP). In order to try to control river flooding, banks are being built, or strengthened, along most of the major rivers across the delta and the flood plain. But they are built to allow 'controlled flooding'. Sluice gates allow 'normal' flood water onto the land to irrigate it, but they keep the excess water in the rivers.

Focus Point 2

Give three reasons why deforestation can increase flooding down-stream.

Give one piece of evidence that suggests deforestation in the Himalayas has **not** caused increased flooding on the Ganges flood plain.

Some people fear that the spread of high-yielding varieties of rice (HYVs), produced by genetic engineering, could result in some of the specialized local varieties being abandoned.

Note Only people with detailed local knowledge can plan properly to make sure that the FAP meets local needs. As with many projects in LEDCs, outsiders can give useful advice – but they must not ignore local knowledge and just tell people what is best for them.

In some areas the FAP is encouraging people to move further away from the river during the flood season. They will only do this if they can grow their crops during the dry season, so the FAP is trying to provide more irrigation water during the dry period.

Other FAP projects include:

- improving flood warning systems

- providing shelters on raised legs, to protect large numbers of people from both river floods and sea floods, caused by cyclones

- raising the mounds that homes are built on, to give extra protection.

In other words, the FAP is helping Bangladeshis to 'live with the floods'.

The subsistence rice growing system

Rice is probably the world's most important food crop. Between one-third and a half of the world's population rely on rice as their staple (main) food. Rice grows best in the monsoon climates of tropical Asia, and over 80 per cent of the world's production is in this region.

Rice grows best with the following inputs from the natural environment:

- a growing season of about 5 months, with temperatures above 21°C

- annual rainfall of over 2000mm, mostly in the growing season

- a dry spell, after the growing season, for harvesting

- flat land, to allow the water to be kept on the fields

- heavy alluvial soils, to provide nutrients

- impermeable soils, to stop the water draining away from the fields.

These conditions are all found on the flood plain of the Ganges. Subsistence farming grew up in this area, based on village units, and this system survived until the late 1950s. Most villages were home to 500–5000 people, including:

- one or two large land-owning families

- several families owning small areas of land

- several families renting land from the large landowners

- landless farmers, who worked for the landowners when possible

- some 'craftsmen families', like blacksmiths, shoemakers and tailors.

Most families farmed on a subsistence basis, each growing enough food for their own use. The larger farmers usually produced a surplus which they sold in the cities, or to visiting merchants. The small farmers produced a surplus in good years, but often they, and the landless farmers, fell into debt in bad years.

There were occasional famines, mainly when monsoon floods were late, but these were usually localized, and did not spread across the whole

Focus Point 3

Cover the page then give four examples of ways that the FAP is helping local people to 'live with the floods'.

Hints and Tips!
Note that in this list of the needs of rice there are no simple statements. Each point has been **elaborated** by adding either a statistic or an explanation. In the exam, simple statements get some marks but you need to elaborate your statements to get the better, high-level marks.

Note When the floods are late, the growing season is cut short. This means that the rice yields are lower than normal. Farmers have to adapt their plans to grow as much as possible in order to survive even in the difficult conditions.

of India. The railway system allowed emergency food supplies to be taken to areas of shortage in all but the worst years.

However, in the 1950s and 1960s the population was seen to be increasing more quickly than it had done in the past. Famine and mass starvation were a very serious threat in India and Bangladesh. The problem was tackled, in two different ways.

- reduce population, or at least slow down the growth, and
- increase food production.

With the help of foreign aid, the main policy was to increase food production through the use of intermediate technology and the more high-technology developments known as the **Green Revolution**.

The Green Revolution in India

The Green Revolution was a group of changes aimed at increasing outputs by increasing inputs. High-tech solutions were developed by scientists, marketed by seed and fertilizer companies, and used by farmers in less economically developed countries.

The Green Revolution was introduced in the Punjab in the 1960s and worked well there because soil conditions were good, irrigation water was freely available and the farmers were already quite well educated and progressive. It has spread to other parts of India, including the Ganges delta, but it has not always been so successful there. Farmers have been slower to take on the new technology, and the systems for providing irrigation water are not so well developed as in the Punjab. However, yields are rising slowly but steadily even in this area.

There has been a lot of discussion about the advantages and disadvantages of the changes. Many people suffered, because they could not compete with the new, more capital-intensive farmers. Many lost their land. Some moved to the cities, but others stayed in the countryside looking for occasional work as landless labourers.

However, it is clear now that the famines that were predicted did not happen. India can feed its population. The Green Revolution has now spread to other parts of India. The ideas have often been spread by education programmes carried on satellite TV channels, which have been made available in most Indian villages. Farmers have become better educated and more willing to accept new ideas. As this has happened birth rates have started to fall in rural areas.

Problems still remain. In particular, there is concern that India's farmers are becoming more dependent on fertilizers, fuel and chemicals made from oil products. This may cause serious long-term problems as these become more scarce but, for now at least, the population is being fed and disaster has been averted.

◆ Not a lot of people realize that India is one of the world's leading countries in terms of use of satellites for TV signals.

◆ It is useful to compare China's one-child policy with India's slower but kinder policy. Their birth rate is falling because people are starting to realize that their living conditions *can* get better, but only if they cut family size.

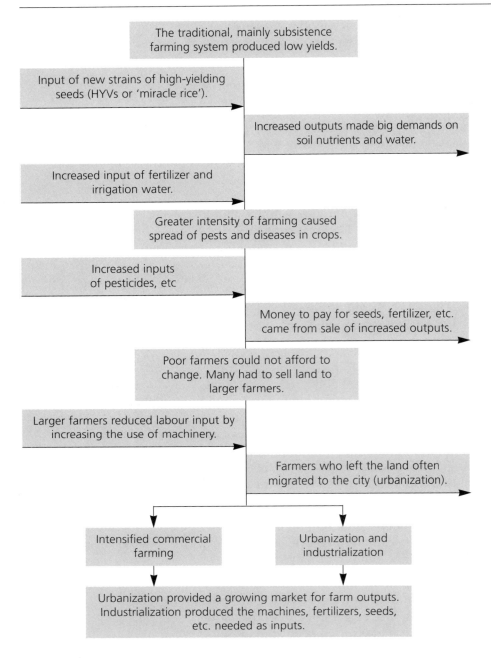

ocus Point 4

Name four inputs needed by the Green Revolution.

Why did the Green Revolution lead to increased urbanization?

ActionAid is a charity based in the UK. It works in Bhola Island in Bangladesh helping people in communities to drill wells for villages. These have to go down 250m to reach layers of sandstone that are saturated with clean, fresh water. Then they install hand pumps to draw the water to the surface.

Intermediate technology and farm development

Intermediate technology (IT) developments are very different from the changes brought by the Green Revolution. The idea of IT was developed by Dr E. F. Schumacher. Writing about how development should take place, he said:

'If you are poor, start with something cheap.
If you are uneducated, start with something fairly simple.
If you are unemployed, start using labour power, because any use of labour is better than letting it lie idle.
A project that does not fit into the environment will be an economic failure and will cause disruption.' ...

'Give a man a fish and you feed him for a day; teach him to fish and he can feed himself for a lifetime.' … 'Teach him to make his own fishing tackle and you have helped him to become self-supporting and independent.' …

Intermediate technology supports:

- not large dams …   … but wells so that people can pump up enough water for their own fields. These are cheaper, land is not lost to flooding, and local people can control them themselves.

- not diesel pumps for the wells …   … but hand-operated pumps, so that local labour is used, rather than expensive, imported fuel. They are also easier to repair, and spare parts can be made in the village.

- not tractors …   … but improved hand tools that can be made from recycled scrap metal by blacksmiths working in the villages.

- not expensive chemical fertilizers …   … but compost made by recycling plant waste and manure.

- not pesticides which pollute the soil …   … but encourage natural predators which eat insects that destroy crops; or teach children to pick pests off the crops.

ocus Point 5

Cover the page. What does intermediate technology support instead of:

- large dams
- diesel pumps
- tractors
- fertilizers
- pesticides?

Exam practice

(a) (i)   How is the land in a delta formed?   (2 marks)

　　(ii) What is a distributary?   (1 mark)

　　(iii) Why does a delta often provide very fertile soil for farming?   (2 marks)

(b) Cyclones often cause severe flooding in the Ganges delta area.

　　(i)   Why have these floods often caused a very high death rate? Refer to:
- the nature of the cyclones
- the relief of the land
- the level of economic development of the area.   (7 marks)

　　(ii) Describe one way in which the governments in the area and/or international relief agencies are trying to reduce the damage caused by cyclones.   (3 marks)

15 B The population of India and Bangladesh

For this topic you should study:
- population, with particular reference to:
  – birth rate, death rate, natural increase in relation to the demographic transition model
  – population structures compared with developed countries
  – population policies, migration to cities, and emigration.

In any study of population you need to know some basic terms.

Birth rate
the number of babies born, for every thousand people in a country, in a year. It is expressed as 'live births/thousand/year' or '‰/year'.

Death rate
the number of people dying out of every thousand in a country, in a year. It is expressed as 'deaths/thousand/year' or '‰/year'.

Natural increase
the difference between the number of births and the number of deaths, in a country, in a year. It is usually expressed as a percentage.

Life expectancy
the average age that people in a country live to be. Separate figures are usually given for males and females.

Infant mortality
the number of babies dying before they reach their fifth birthday. This figure is usually given per thousand population (‰).

Hints and Tips!

Learn these five definitions precisely.

Basic population statistics are given below for India and Bangladesh. Figures for the UK are also given for comparison.

	Birth rate (per 1000)	Death rate (per 1000)	Natural increase %	Life expectancy Male (years)	Life expectancy Female (years)	Infant mortality (per 1000)
India	29	10	1.9	57	59	87
Bangladesh	36	13	2.3	54	52	118
UK	14	11	0.3	73	79	7

Hints and Tips!

It is not essential to know the exact figures in this table, but you should be able to recognize the figures for birth rate, death rate, etc. for an LEDC and an MEDC. Of course, if you *can* learn the figures without spending too much time on them, it might be useful in your exam.

The demographic transition model

In many countries it has been observed that, as the economy develops, the population structure goes through a series of changes. These changes are called the **demographic transition**.

Stage 1

In countries with very simple, subsistence economies, health care is usually poor. This means that the death rate is high, especially amongst the most vulnerable group – babies and children under five.

Couples usually have many babies, hoping that one or two will survive, so the birth rate is also high.

A high birth rate and a high death rate means that the population stays low. It may fall suddenly in bad years of drought, famine or disease. Then it may rise slowly again as conditions improve, only to fall again when the next difficult time arrives.

Both India and Bangladesh have passed through this stage. Their death rate is now much lower than in Stage 1.

Stage 2

As the economy starts to develop, money becomes available for better health care – doctors, nurses, medicines, better sanitation, drier and warmer housing, better pre- and post-natal care, etc. This means death rate starts to fall, slowly at first, then faster as conditions improve. Usually birth rate stays high, because people are used to having many children. It takes time to change the 'culture of the high birth rate'.

The high birth rate and falling death rate combine to cause population increase. It starts growing slowly, but the rate of growth speeds up. This can cause a 'population explosion'.

Bangladesh and India both entered this stage in the 1950s/1960s. Bangladesh is still in this stage – see the graph above.

Stage 3

People keep on having large numbers of children as long as they feel there is a need for them. Reasons for a high birth rate include:

- children can support parents in their old age

- children can work on farms, in industry or in services. Their wages can make the difference between survival and disaster for families.

So the birth rate starts to fall when people no longer feel that they *need* to have large families. In other words, it falls as the standard of living of the poor people starts to rise.

In this stage the death rate is low, and although the birth rate is falling it is still higher than the death rate. The population total still grows, but the rate of growth slows down.

India is probably in Stage 3 now. The birth rate has started to fall. It is still rather high, but it is quite a lot lower than in Bangladesh. Actually this overall figure hides variations. The birth rate in the cities is usually lower than the rate in the countryside. If figures were available to

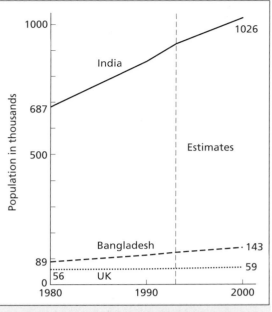

▲ *Population changes, 1980–2000 (est.)*

◆ In the 1960s the world's population increased very rapidly. This was not because people had started to have many more children –it was because fewer people were dying.

◆ Contraceptives and family planning advice alone will not cut the birth rate. It only falls when couples realize *they* can benefit by not having big families.

compare the birth rates in Calcutta and in the rice-growing areas of the delta, they would probably show that Calcutta is well into Stage 3 but the rural areas are still in Stage 2.

Stage 4

In most MEDCs birth and death rates are both low. Health care is good and reliable. People expect their children to survive, so they keep families small. In fact, in more wealthy countries children have become very expensive, because people expect to pay for them to have a high standard of housing, food, leisure, etc. People have a strong **motive** to limit their families, and family planning gives them the **means** to do this.

In MEDCs, with a low birth and death rate, the total population is steady. Total population is often high, but these countries have a strong economy, which can support the large numbers. The graph shows that the UK is now in Stage 4.

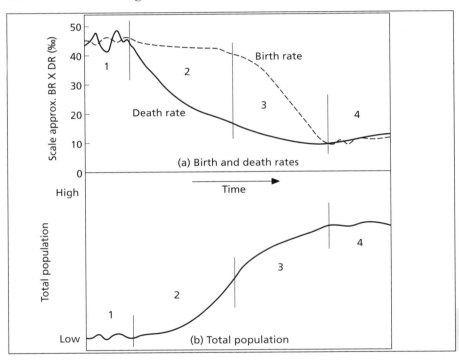

In Stage 3 the population increase slows down – but population is still rising. Unfortunately students often get confused about this and say that population starts to fall. BE CAREFUL! Do not make this mistake.

◀ *The demographic transition model*

Population structures

So far in this chapter we have looked at population totals and changes in total population. Geographers also need to look at the **structure** of the population. This means examining how the population can be divided up into different groups, based on age and sex. The usual way of showing this information is on a **population pyramid**.

In the pyramids below, each bar represents an age/sex group. Males are shown on the left and females on the right; young people are at the bottom and old people at the top. The length of the bar shows the percentage of the total population in that group. For instance, in India 13.7% of the total population is male, from 0–9 years old.

Population control

Careful study of the details of the demographic transition model above should make one thing clear. *It seems as though the most reliable way to reduce the birth rate is to raise people's standard of living.* There are many reasons why poor peasant farmers need to have many children.

- Children can work on the farm from a very early age. Even 6 and 7-year-olds can help to scare birds or weed the crops.

- Children are needed to support their parents in old age. There are no old age pensions.

- With the high death rate, parents feel that they need to have many children so that they can be sure that at least one will survive.

ocus Point 1

Study the annotations that have been marked on the UK pyramid. Re-read the information in this chapter then study the pyramids for India and Bangladesh carefully. Annotate them to point out and explain the main features of their population structures.

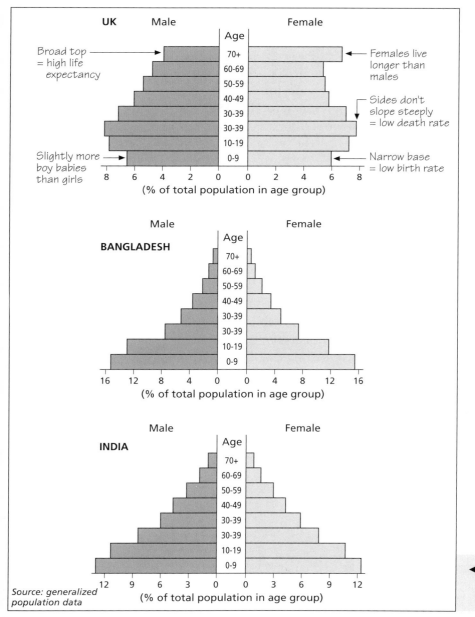

Source: generalized population data

◀ *Population pyramids for India, Bangladesh and the UK*

- At least one of the children may be able to get work in a city and send money home to support the family.

- People take great pride in their families, and sons often play an important part in religious ceremonies, including the Hindu funeral ceremonies.

In India there have been several big campaigns to try to encourage people to use contraception. The government and aid agencies tried various policies.

- Advertising the benefits of smaller families, using posters, TV and even, in one famous example, painting slogans on the side of elephants and leading them round villages.

- Giving away free contraceptives – but this is no use unless couples want to use them and know how to use them. Contraceptive education is difficult in areas where many people are illiterate and the education of women is especially poor.

- Encouraging men to be sterilized, at first by persuasion, and then by forcing some men to be sterilized. This caused widespread opposition, and was one reason why the government of the time was voted out of power. Democratic India would not accept the kind of policies that had worked in China.

- Recently it has been found that the best way to cut the birth rate is to educate and support women. In particular to:

  – provide good health care for women and their children

  – encourage literacy, so that women can read advice on health care, contraception, good diet, and so on

  – raise the status of women, so they can control their own lives and make decisions about their families.

There is now clear evidence that India's population growth is starting to slow down. This is happening fastest in the cities and in those rural areas where the farming is most developed. Unfortunately, the growth rate is still high in Bangladesh. The country is poorer, with less money to spend on health care and education.

Migration to cities

Conditions in rural areas put a lot of pressures on the inhabitants to leave the countryside and migrate to the cities. These pressures are sometimes called **pushes**. The diagram below shows some of them.

Focus Point 2

Cover up the page. Give at least four reasons why poor farming families in India and Bangladesh need to have a lot of children.

Focus Point 3

Cover the page. List three ways of working with women to help create the right conditions that will lead to a fall in the birth rate.

Pushes	Pulls
• Shortage of farmland and food caused by the growing population. • Loss of jobs on the land caused by mechanization of farming. • Loss of land caused when poor farmers fall into debt. • Constant threat of disasters caused by flood, wind, monsoon failure, etc. • Lack of opportunity for jobs and prosperity. • Lack of opportunity for education, etc.	

ocus Point 4

At the same time, the cities often **pull** people towards them. Complete the second half of this diagram by listing some of the pull factors that attract people to Calcutta. Many of these are mentioned in the next chapter.

◀ *Countryside to cities: push and pull factors*

Exam practice

(a) The population of the rural areas of the Ganges delta has a high birth rate.

   (i) Give two reasons to explain why the birth rate is so high in this area.   (4 marks)

   (ii) Some people say that the best way to cut the birth rate is to improve health care for babies and children. Why is this so?   (2 marks)

(b) (i) Complete this table to show changes during the demographic transition. (You may use words from the list below, but Higher-level candidates should not need to use them.)

Stage	1	2	3	4
Death rate				
Birth rate				
Total population				

(8 marks)

- high • high • high but now stable • low • low • low
- rising at an increasing rate • starts to fall • starts to fall • stays high
- still falling • still rising, but at slower rate

   (ii) Explain what causes the change from Stage 2 to Stage 3 of the demographic transition.   (2 marks)

   (iii) Explain what causes the change from Stage 3 to Stage 4.   (2 marks)

15 C Calcutta

For this topic you should study:
- Calcutta, with particular reference to:
  - its location and morphology (land formation)
  - migration from rural areas
  - population structure
  - problems of the city and attempted solutions.

Calcutta, which has a population of about 10 million, is India's second largest city after Bombay, now known as Mumbai (about 14 million). New Delhi, the capital, has about 6 million people.

Calcutta lies on the Hooghly River, which is one of the distributaries carrying water from the Ganges, into the Bay of Bengal. It lies over 100km from the coast, but the Hooghly is so wide that ocean-going boats can reach the city. Calcutta lies on the eastern (left) bank of the river, and forms a conurbation with Howrah on the right bank.

There was a very important trading city and port here in 1757, when the British seized it. They wanted Calcutta so that they could control the trade of Bengal. The area of Bengal probably had around 40 million inhabitants, and the farmers produced a surplus of crops, especially cotton and jute, which were traded for British manufactured goods.

Bengal was the name given to a state that was independent before the British arrived. East Bengal is now the country of Bangladesh. West Bengal is now part of India.

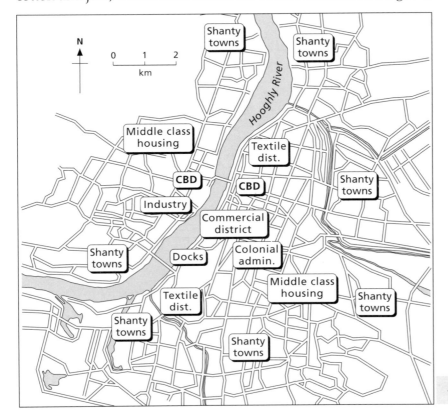

Jute is a plant that produces fibres used to make sacks and rope.

◀ *Urban zones of Calcutta*

Once the British controlled the city, their merchants built docks, warehouses, company offices, large houses, etc. in the central area. Nearby were the palaces and public buildings of the Indian rulers. The Indian commercial and small industrial areas were further back from the river. They were surrounded by the homes of the people who worked in the city. Calcutta was an important trading port, and it grew steadily. When the British left India in 1947, it had about 2 million people!

The state of Bengal was divided into two parts. West Bengal, whose people were mostly Hindus, became part of India, and East Bengal, whose people were mostly Muslims, became part of Pakistan. Many Muslims from West Bengal migrated to East Bengal, and non-Muslims (mainly Hindus) moved the other way. Most of the migrants into India could not find land of their own, so many of them came as refugees to Calcutta.

Many of the refugees set up shanty towns on spare land around the outskirts of Calcutta. Others were forced to live on the pavements in the city centre, moving to live on railway station platforms, in bus shelters and in the entrance halls of large buildings during the monsoon rains.

Since 1947 there have been further influxes of refugees caused by:

- droughts and floods in the region
- people being forced off the land by the commercialization of agriculture after the Green Revolution in the 1960s and '70s
- population pressure caused by a high birth rate and falling death rate.

Each new group is pulled to Calcutta by the hope of finding work and shelter. Many of the newcomers have friends and family in Calcutta already, and they look to them for help to get established in the city. Then, even if they cannot find work, they have more chance to make a living by begging in a big city than they could in the countryside.

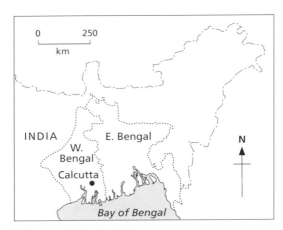

Before partition in 1947

West Bengal - mainly Hindu, also many Muslims

East Bengal - mainly Muslim, also many Hindus

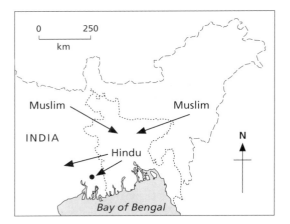

After partition

←——— Population movement

◀ *The partition of Bengal*

Population structure

In the 1960s, when migration into Calcutta was at its peak, the population structure of the immigrant population was very uneven.

The majority of the migrants were men of working age: 68 per cent of the people on the pyramid are males aged between 10 and 45. Some just came to Calcutta temporarily. They sent money back to their families in the villages, and returned when they had finished working. Others settled, and brought their families to join them later. Temporary migrants mainly lived in very rough accommodation; it was not worth spending money on their homes. The others, who intended to stay, often put a lot of effort into setting up a home for their family.

Growth of the shanty towns ('bustees' in Calcutta)

Each new group of migrants either moves to the pavements in the centre, or to spare areas of land on the outskirts. To people from MEDCs, conditions in these settlements looks appalling – but it is vital that you understand why and how these settlements developed.

Most people are attracted to Calcutta by opportunity. Many cannot get formal jobs, but they can make a living in the informal sector. (This does not just mean shoe shining. It includes a great variety of work, buying and selling, making and mending, servicing and recycling.) The chances of an education for their children offer a further opportunity for the family to get on. People in this situation have to be flexible and adapt to change if they are to prosper. They need a home, not luxury.

Many GCSE students write about 'spontaneous settlements' with a very stereotyped view of the squalor and poverty. They often miss out reasons for the conditions that they describe.

Most new settlements are gradually improved as people can afford to buy materials and improve their homes. The Calcutta Metropolitan Development Authority (CMDA) is responsible for improving conditions in the city. This is happening slowly but surely. Its priority is to provide services, not to improve the houses: that must be left to the occupiers. Since the 1960s the CMDA has:

- improved sewage disposal – in the 1960s there were 1000 deaths a year from cholera but in recent years there have been none

- improved water supply – there is now a tap for every 25 slum houses

- made concrete roads to replace mud tracks between the shacks

- installed street lights in many shanty towns, to improve safety, and to give some light for people with no electricity in their home

- tried to improve the traffic flow by widening roads and improving public transport. Despite the improvements the traffic system is still very overcrowded (but that problem is not unique to Calcutta).

Hints and Tips!

In the exam, do not just say 'they came to work'. What kind of work did they look for? You know Calcutta has docks and industries, shops and offices. There would be some jobs there, but most new migrants would have to look for very menial work – street cleaning, sorting and recycling rubbish, selling things on the street, domestic work, and so on.

Hints and Tips!

In other words, the pushes from the countryside have got weaker, and the pulls to Calcutta have also got weaker.

The CMDA's job has become easier because migration to the city has slowed down. The city's population is now growing by only 0.4 per cent per year (compared with 7 per cent in Bombay). This is due to:

- Industry is developing in other towns nearby, in the Damodar Valley, providing another attraction to migrants.

- It is now known that Calcutta cannot provide jobs for new migrants and this discourages people who were thinking of moving there.

- Conditions in the countryside have improved. The Green Revolution has improved yields and raised rural living standards.

Focus Point 1

Cover up the page.

Give five negative stereotypes of spontaneous settlements.

Give the reasons why settlements develop like this.

Negative stereotype	Actual reasons
• Houses are poorly built, often using scrap materials.	• Money is in short supply. It has to be spent on food, or invested in tools or materials for work.
• Houses seem to be poorly planned, with bits tacked on.	• Homes have to provide a place for the family to sleep and eat – and the family may change size as children are born or leave to work elsewhere. Also, people from the home village may need support when they arrive in the city.
• There are no proper windows, and walls are very flimsy.	• Calcutta is in the tropics. Ventilation is more important than insulation.
• The houses do not have proper toilets and sewers.	• These are expensive and complicated. They may be provided in the future, but people often make pit latrines which are emptied by tank lorries every few months.
• They do not have electricity.	• Once settlements are established the authorities may link them to the supply – but it is difficult to keep up with the rapid growth.
• There are no roads, only dirt tracks.	• Not many people own cars. It is more important to have access to a bus route to the city centre.
• The area looks a mess.	• Many people are carrying on their jobs in and around their homes. Builders have to store materials, some keep animals for food, others make things from recycled scrap to sell, and so on. Opportunity is more important than tidiness.

Exam practice

Many people from rural areas in the Ganges delta migrate to Calcutta. Give two push factors and two pull factors that help to cause this migration.   (4 marks)

Hints and Tips!

You should try not to use stereotypes when you describe spontaneous settlements. Learn precise facts about the CMDA and then you can describe a real place, not just a stereotype slum.

Focus Point 2

Cover the page.

List five improvements that the CMDA has made to life in the shanty towns of Calcutta. Remember, though, that as they improve conditions in one settlement, another one is probably starting to develop somewhere else in the city.

16 | Japan

> **For this topic you should study:**
> - the main physical features, and constraints on the distribution of population and industry
> - location of natural resources
> - production of manufactured goods, with particular reference to:
>   - the influence of raw materials and energy on the distribution of motor vehicle, electrical goods and high-tech industries
>   - the role of automation and mass production in Japan's economic growth
>   - environmental damage and pollution, and attempted solutions to the problems
> - trade, with particular reference to:
>   - Japan's balance of trade and trends in Japan's trade
>   - outward investment into the European Union
>   - trade with the Pacific Rim and South-east Asia.

Japan's main physical features and population distribution

Japan lies on the margin between the Pacific Plate and the Eurasian Plate. This is a destructive margin, where the denser Pacific Plate is being forced down beneath the continental Eurasian Plate. This violent movement causes earthquakes and volcanoes which have formed the mountains of Japan.

The friction between the plates also generates heat. This can cause the ocean plate to melt as it sinks down into the mantle. The melting produces a reservoir of magma (molten rock) beneath the Earth's crust. Sometimes the pressure on this magma forces it upwards, through a crack in the crust. Then it spills out at the surface as a volcano.

Mountains, deep river valleys and the rocky, unstable coastline make large parts of Japan unsuitable for human settlement. Only 17 per cent of the land is suitable for dense settlement and industry. This is almost all found on the narrow coastal strip. Settlements are particularly concentrated around the bays and inlets which form sheltered harbours, because so many people depend on the industries that have grown up there, based on imported raw materials.

The bays also provide some shelter from tsunamis and typhoons, which are other natural hazards that threaten Japan. **Tsunamis** are great waves, set off by earthquakes on the sea bed. They can affect any part of Japan, but especially the east coast. **Typhoon** is the local name for tropical storms, similar to the cyclones in the Bay of Bengal (see page 115). Typhoons are common in Kyushu and southern Honshu.

There is no English word for 'tsunami'. These waves are sometimes called 'tidal waves', but they have nothing to do with the tides, so it is better just to borrow from the Japanese and call them tsunami.

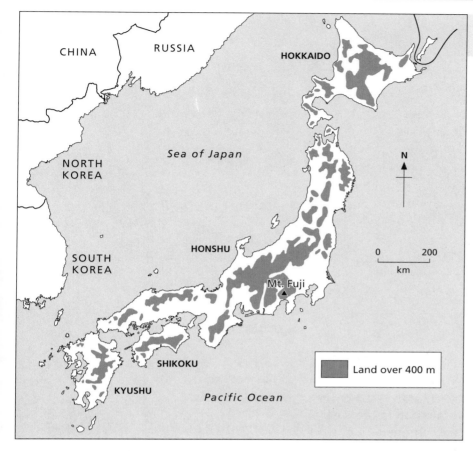

◀ *Japan's physical features*

Hints and Tips!

◆ To help remember why there are earthquakes at plate margins think of the three stages:

1 **Movement** caused by convection current.

2 **Friction** between the plates.

3 **Sudden slip** when pressure builds up, causes earthquake.

◆ To help remember why volcanoes erupt at plate margins, think of three stages:

1 Heavier plate **sinks** as they move together.

2 Sinking plate **melts** due to friction and heating.

3 **Pressure build-up** causes eruption.

Japan's natural resources

Compared with other major industrial countries, Japan is very short of natural resources. For instance:

- **Coal** – When the country first started to industrialize in the late nineteenth century, there were some small, poor deposits in the south of the country and on Hokkaido, but now these are just about exhausted.

- **Oil and gas** – Some fields have also been found on Honshu, but these have never been important.

- **HEP** – Japan's high mountains, steep slopes and reliable rainfall, all favour HEP. Unfortunately, none of the river basins is large enough to allow the development of major schemes. HEP provides 7 per cent of Japan's electricity at present, but this is unlikely to increase. The biggest HEP scheme is on the Kurobe River.

- **Geothermal power** – At present, 5 per cent of Japan's electricity comes from geothermal schemes . Many of the rocks below the surface are hot, so there is a lot of potential for further development.

- **Alternative power** – Like Britain, Japan is an island, surrounded by seas where strong winds blow, waves are high and the range of the tides in some of the bays is great. All of this offers potential for

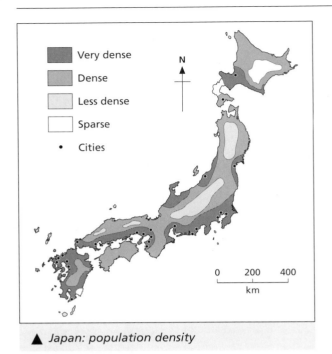

▲ *Japan: population density*

Very dense
Dense
Less dense
Sparse
• Cities

N

0   200   400
km

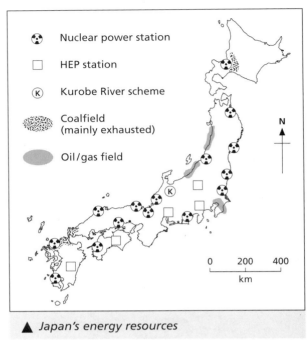

▲ *Japan's energy resources*

◉ Nuclear power station
☐ HEP station
Ⓚ Kurobe River scheme
▨ Coalfield (mainly exhausted)
▨ Oil/gas field

N

0   200   400
km

generation of electricity in the twenty-first century. It has not been developed yet, but Japan may prove to have better energy resources in the next century than it has had in the past!

Manufacturing industry in Japan

From reading the previous section you will realize that most of Japan's raw materials for industry have to be imported.

Japan could only industrialize by making sure that:

- it could afford to pay for the imports by exporting lots of goods
- its exports were high value compared with low-value imports
- it controlled the sources of supply of its imports.

To control supplies of essential raw materials, Japan often invested in mines, railways and ports in other countries.

You should now be able to work out two main reasons why Japanese industry is concentrated around the coast:

	Imports what it needs
Uranium	100%
Iron ore (although now a lot of scrap is reused)	100%
Oil	99.8%
Gas	99.5%
Hard wood	95%
Coal	88%

An example of Japanese investment in other countries to provide raw materials for Japan's industry is the iron ore mine at Mt Tom Price in the north-west of Australia. This was built entirely by the Japanese, and all the ore is exported to Japan.

Focus Point 1

Cover up the page. Give the two main reasons why Japan's industry is concentrated around the coast.

- Most people live close to the coast because of the flat land. These people provide the workforce and the market.

- Most raw materials are brought in through the ports, so transport costs are reduced if the factory is close to the coast.

Industry is concentrated in the four main industrial zones shown on the map.

The motor industry

In Japan there are two parts to the motor industry:

- A few very large, highly automated, capital-intensive assembly plants. The locations of the main plants are shown on the map to the right.

- Many small, more labour-intensive component manufacturers. They are mostly found in the main industrial areas, but others are scattered throughout the country.

For example, many firms in the Kobe region make parts for larger firms throughout Japan. The country's efficient transport system means that these parts can be delivered very quickly, 'just in time' to be used in production. Big firms therefore do not need to hold large stocks of parts. One unexpected result of the Kobe earthquake in 1995 was the damage done to the motor industry. The earthquake disrupted many of Kobe's firms, and the whole region's transport system. Without parts from Kobe, many of the big factories had to stop work for several weeks, even months.

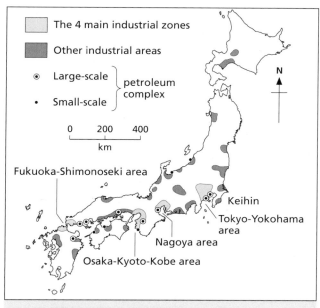

▲ Japan's industrial zones

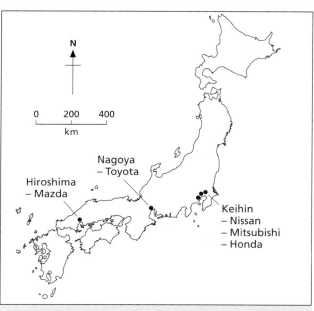

▲ Location of Japan's major car assembly plants

The motor industry uses steel as its main raw material, so the main engine and body plants are located close to steel works, which are close to the ports. New car assembly plants are often built on land that has been reclaimed from the sea, because of the shortage of suitable flat land.

The electrical and high-tech industries

Refer back to the section on 'High-technology industry in the M4 corridor' on page 42. This makes the point that high-tech industry can be divided into two sections. These deal with research and development, and mass production of the goods. Exactly the same situation can be found in Japan's high-tech industry.

Stage 1 – research and development   The electronics, optical (cameras, etc.) and computer industries in Japan are enormous, and play a vital part in their economy. The high-tech sector first developed in the late 1950s and 1960s. Then the Japanese took ideas that had been developed in the West and used them efficiently to make more profits than the people who had the original ideas. Now, a lot of the profits made by the big firms are re-invested in research and development.

Stage 2 – manufacturing in Japan   Once the ideas have been developed, the products are built in other parts of Japan. As with the motor industry, large corporations build assembly plants, usually near big cities, close to labour and the market. The components are made in small factories and workshops scattered around the country.

Stage 3 – manufacturing overseas   Labour in Japan is expensive, and it is likely to become more expensive. Skilled workers expect good wages and benefits. They can demand good conditions, because there is a growing shortage of workers as the population ages. The population pyramid overleaf shows how low birth and death rates have led to this.

The big corporations try to cut down costs by:

- mechanization – replacing workers with machinery

- encouraging hard work from the labour force – providing good conditions, but expecting dedicated work in exchange.

In spite of this it is difficult to stay competitive with countries where labour costs are lower. As a result Japanese corporations are now building factories overseas. Once they have shown that their production processses can be successful and their goods are profitable, the major electronic firms produce most of their goods in countries

Focus Point 2

Describe three stages in the location of the Japanese high-tech industry. Use these headings:

1 Research and development
2 Early production
3 Later, mass production

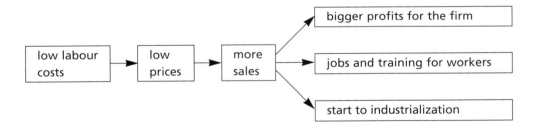

where labour is cheaper. Many 'Japanese' electronic goods – computers, game consoles and so on – are actually assembled in countries like Malaysia and Thailand – the 'tiger economies'. In the late 1990s they are spreading into even poorer countries, such as Bangladesh and India. This leads to:

Japanese industry and the environment

The rapid development of industry in a small, crowded country, where only a small percentage of the land is suitable for settlement, has led to many environmental problems. The Japanese, as might be expected, have shown great ingenuity in attempting to tackle the problems.

Hints and Tips!

Learn the list of problems first. Once you know them it is far easier to learn the solutions, because you have a structure to help your learning.

Exhaustion of fuel resources.	Development of nuclear power and HEP. Research into alternatives, like solar and geothermal power.
Deforestation of Japan's countryside.	Replanting of forest on steep slopes. Setting up National Parks to conserve remaining forests.
Shortage of land for industry	Building new land into the sea, often using rubbish to fill in part of the site.
Pollution of lakes and rivers by waste spills and dumping.	Strict new laws on factory emissions, and on dumping of waste by oil tankers. Investment in new technology to recycle waste.

Japan's trade

In 1990 Japan had a trade surplus with the rest of the world of $63 billion. That means the Japanese exported goods worth $63 billion more than the goods they imported. This 'positive balance of trade', repeated over many years, meant that Japan had built up an enormous reserve of foreign currency. It gave them great power in world markets.

On the other hand it caused a lot of resentment in other industrialized countries. The EU and the USA felt that Japan put up many barriers to imports. For instance, they put very high taxes on Scotch whisky, but fairly low taxes on Japanese whisky. Also they often turned away imports because of some small problem with filling in the very complicated paperwork that they demanded.

To try to stop the bad feelings the Japanese started building factories in other countries. The Japanese call this 'outward investment'. The countries where the money is invested call it 'inward investment'.

Investment in the European Union
A lot of the profits made by Japanese corporations have been invested in the European Union. There are several reasons for this.

- The EU put limits on the number of cars that could be imported from Japan. If the cars are assembled in the EU the limits do not apply.

- In parts of the EU (including UK), labour costs are lower than in Japan.

- The governments offered incentives, such as grants to help with building costs, and tax reductions.

There were many advantages to the countries where these factories were built.

- The factories employed workers in areas of high unemployment.

- Components were made in other factories nearby, bringing more jobs.

- There was a cut in imports. This helped the balance of payments.

DID YOU KNOW?

One of the new industrial techniques that the Japanese brought to the UK is the 'just in time' delivery system. This means parts are delivered very efficiently, just in time to be used. The company can save money by not having to store large amounts of parts, just in case they are needed, as they had done in the past.

- Many of the firms gave very good training to their workers, improving the country's level of skills.

- Japanese management techniques produced very efficient factories. Other companies in the area could learn from these.

A large proportion of Japanese inward investment into the EU has come to the UK. For example, the motor industry has built a lot of factories in old industrial regions: Nissan built a large plant in Washington, Tyne and Wear. Toyota built an assembly plant in Derbyshire, and an engine plant at Deeside in North Wales. Honda are in Swindon. South Wales and Central Scotland, also areas of high unemployment, are now home to many Japanese electrical firms.

Trade with the Pacific Rim

For most of the twentieth century the main area of world trade was the Atlantic. Trade between West European countries, and their trade with the USA and Canada, dominated the world trade in manufactured goods. In the 1980s trade between nations on the Pacific Rim became greater than the Atlantic trade. There were several causes.

- The economy of the west coast of the USA had grown spectacularly since the 1920s. California was the most important area of growth, but the north-west coast is now important too.

- Silicon Valley in California, and Seattle, home of the Microsoft Corporation, are both high-tech industrial areas on the Pacific coast.

- Japan's economy has grown enormously since the 1950s.

- The 'tiger economies' in South Korea, Singapore, Hong Kong, etc. have grown rapidly since the 1960s, helped by Japanese investments.

- Other countries such as Malaysia, Thailand, Indonesia and Vietnam have started to industrialize too, following the example of the 'tigers'.

- China is starting to become part of the world economy, and to trade with other countries. As China is home to a quarter of the world's people there will be enormous opportunities for more trade if the 'opening up' continues.

However, since the end of 1997 the Asian economies have had problems. The rapid growth of the 'tigers' was based on large-scale borrowing of money. Several countries are having difficulty paying back their debts. South Korea, Indonesia, Malaysia and some others are having to negotiate with the World Bank to get new loans.

Their economies have suffered. There has been a sudden, rapid increase in unemployment. Many immigrant workers are being deported, because there is no work for them. Problems in one country are having 'knock-on' effects in other countries, because trade is being cut back.

Economists say that Japan is the one country that can help to reduce the problem for the rest of the Pacific Rim. The developing economies and

DID YOU KNOW?

Malaysia, Thailand, Indonesia and Vietnam are sometimes called the 'baby tigers'!

the 'tigers' can only keep their industry going if Japan, the one developed country in the region, buys more of their products. If Japan opens up its trade and lets more imports into the country the crisis may be only a short-term problem. If Japan keeps its protection systems in place the crisis may become a disaster.

Exam practice

(a) *Either* Why does Japan suffer many earthquakes?

   Or Why does Japan have many active and dormant volcanoes? (3 marks)

(b) (i) Name two important forms of energy for which Japan has to rely on importing most of its supplies. (1 mark)

   (ii) Name two alternative (renewable) sources of energy that Japan can produce for itself (or may soon be able to produce). (1 mark)

   (iii) Choose one of the sources of alternative energy named in (ii) above. Explain why the land of Japan is suitable for production of this type of energy. (3 marks)

(c) (i) Name one of Japan's major industrial regions and mark it on an outline map of the country. (1 mark)

   (ii) Give two reasons to explain why most of Japan's industry is located on the coast. (4 marks)

   (iii) In the past, Japanese industry had a reputation for copying other people's ideas and not developing its own. This is no longer true. Explain what the Japanese are doing to encourage research and development (R&D) for industry. (2 marks)

(d) (i) Name two countries on the Pacific Rim (other than Japan) which are important trading partners with Japan. (1 mark)

   (ii) Give two reasons to explain why Japanese firms have built many assembly plants in other countries in recent years. (4 marks)

Answers and advice on the Exam Questions

1 Urban growth and change (page 15)

Note how this question is laid out. At the start of (a) you are told to name a town. Then there is a series of questions labelled (i) to (iv). The town that you name has to be used to illustrate your answers to **all** parts of (a). Before you rush into your answer, read the whole of question (a). This will help you choose your town or city wisely. Try to be sure that you can answer all four sections using information about the town you choose. You should be very careful that your town can be used for part (iv) – because that section has most marks!

Then, at the start of (b), there is another instruction. The area that you have to name here must be used for all parts of (b). However, the town that you named in (a) does not have to be used here. The way the question is laid out means that the first instruction 'Name an industrial town or city ...' only applies to (a).

(a) (ii) Note that there are 2 marks available for this answer, but you are only asked for one reason. This quite clearly means that you must develop or elaborate your answer. A single phrase is not enough.

e.g. 'It had to be on a coalfield for power.' This would only get 1 mark because it only has one simple idea.

'It had to be on a coalfield because it needed a source of power, and coal was so bulky that it would have been too expensive to transport it a long distance.' This would easily gain the second mark because the reason is explained in some detail.

(iii) Again you need to elaborate your answer for full marks.

e.g. 'The houses were packed close together as near as possible to the docks.' One idea gets 1 mark.

'The houses were built in the area called Byker. They were packed close together as near as possible to the docks.' Here a good, named example is given, and this precision gains the extra mark.

(iv) There are two parts to this question, and 4 marks. Write clearly elaborated and developed points to describe both the houses and the street pattern.

e.g. 'The workers' houses in Salford were brick-built terraced houses and most of them had two rooms downstairs and two bedrooms. Many of them did not have inside toilets but just a privy at the bottom of the yard. The streets were usually laid out in a rectangular pattern with people's front doors opening straight onto the pavement.'

(b) Your answer will depend on the area that you have chosen. However, you must try to develop your points in detail. There are 4 marks for each section, so the examiner will expect extended writing and logical development of ideas. Precise references to the chosen area are also needed.

(c) e.g. 'London is a perfect example of a city with commuter villages and towns. They developed because many people worked in the city but could afford to live out in the countryside and then travel to work by car, train or underground. Lilley near Luton is a commuter village with lovely big houses in an unpolluted environment.'

2 The farm as a system (page 22)

(a) (i) Note that **all** you are asked for here is a diagram. You are not asked for any extended writing, but you need to add clear written labels to your diagram. Drawing diagrams is an important skill that you should practise carefully. Check the diagram on page 19 of this book. Make sure that you have learnt it precisely.

(ii) You could answer this questions with a diagram or extended writing. In a geography exam you will always get credit for using relevant technical terms. Here, the obvious term to use is 'rain shadow'. If you have not used that term in your answer, make sure that you know it. Use it next time!

(b) Before you can explain you probably need to give a brief description of the relief of the two areas. The obvious point to make here is that the steep slopes in the Lake District are not suitable for the machines used by arable farmers, but the gentle slopes of East Anglia are suitable. That alone will not get the full 5 marks. You need to think about this **geographically**.

Steep slopes often have thin soils, because rainwater washes the soil down (erosion). Thicker soils can develop on gentle slopes. If you can think through points like this and make connections between different aspects of the physical and human geography of an area, you will gain high marks.

(c) This question contains two 'command words': **describe** and **explain**.

Describe tells you to say *what* is there. To do this you need carefully learnt knowledge about a real place.

Explain tells you to say *why* it is there. Here you need to develop ideas and show how things are linked together. In this part of your answer you need to show connections. Use phrases like:
'If the farmer does this he will benefit because ...'
'Doing this is good for the soil because ...'
'Growing these crops reduces the costs and increases profits because ...'

3 Electricity generation (page 29)

(a) Check your answers with the map on page 28.

(b) If you chose the Trent valley you could say:

'This area is close to the Notts coalfield and close to the River Trent for water supply.' This would probably gain you 2 marks. To gain the full 4 marks you could write:

'This area is close to the Notts coalfield so the cost of transporting bulky fuel to the power stations is reduced. Power stations are built along the River Trent so they have plenty of water for cooling the steam so that it can be recycled.' In other words, **develop** and **elaborate** your points.

(c) Refer to some of the following: high rainfall, low evaporation, large catchment area, steep slopes, narrow valleys for dams, impermeable rocks, cheap land for reservoirs, etc. Once again, try to develop and elaborate the simple ideas listed.

(d) When nuclear stations were first being developed they were built in remote areas (e.g. Calder Hall, Dounreay) for safety reasons. Later stations (e.g. Hartlepool, Dungeness) were built closer to cities because it was cheaper to transport the electricity over short distances.

(e) Emphasize the benefits of the new sources and the problems associated with the old ones, e.g. acid rain, greenhouse gases, exhaustion of resources, rising costs, etc.

4 River systems in the hydrological cycle (page 38)

(a) The three parts of (a) are all linked, but each part needs different skills. You must name a real example in (i) but make sure you choose an example that you can describe in enough detail to gain 3 marks in (ii). When you describe the feature try to show 'a sense of place'. Describe a real place, not a diagram. If possible, describe somewhere you have been and studied in the field. If that is not possible, describe an example that you have seen in photos or on videos.

In (iii) you need to be more theoretical. The 'command' part of (iii) tells you to 'use one or more diagrams'. You can also include extended writing, or you can put your explanations as labels on the diagram. It is very important that you know how to draw these diagrams quickly but accurately. The best way to make sure you can do this is to get plenty of practice. Select some of the diagrams and maps from this book and draw them as often as you can. Each time you should get better, quicker and more detailed. Learning the diagram should help you to learn a set of ideas and to visualize how different processes and/or places are linked together.

(b) (i) The key points here are
   • the basin structure of the rocks
   • the presence of a permeable layer of rock between two impermeable layers
   • rainfall from the Chilterns and South Downs percolating through the chalk
   • wells being drilled down to the water table.

   Again, learning the diagram should help you to understand and learn all these points.

   (ii) The Thames; purified, recycled water.

(c) There are many possible examples. It is probably best for you to learn details of your own local example.

5 A Manufacturing industry (page 44)

(a) (i) Estuaries provide sheltered ports for importing raw materials and exporting finished goods. Rivers provide a source of fresh water for industrial processes and cleaning.

   (ii) Tees, Thames, Southampton Water, Avon, Mersey. (These are the main ones.)

(b) Check your answers with page 41 in this book, or your own notes. You will need knowledge like this if you are aiming for a high grade. The only way to make sure of this knowledge is by hard learning.

(c) The key idea here is that the waste materials of one chemical plant often become the raw materials for another. Explain and illustrate that idea by referring to named examples of plants, the raw materials that each uses, and the finished products that are manufactured there.

(d) Refer to some of the following:
   • Good transport links, especially motorways and airports.
   • The knowledge base of the area in universities and research establishments.
   • The close links between firms in the high-tech sector.
   • The large, rich market nearby – London, the South East, Midlands, Europe.

   • The attractive environment encourages skilled workers to move into the area.

   Try to give the name of a place, an area or a firm to illustrate each point that you make.

6 Leisure and tourism in the UK (page 58)

(a) To conserve unspoilt countryside, and to encourage access. Both parts for 1 mark. These are basic ideas that **must** be learnt.

(b) (i) Before you choose the feature, make sure you **read the whole question**. There is only 1 mark for choosing the feature, but 7 marks for what you write about it!

   (ii) **Describe** just means 'say what it looks like'. For 2 marks you need some detail, but do not explain *why* it is like that.

   (iii) Here explanation *is* needed. Questions about glacial processes mean abrasion and plucking. Learn about them!

   When the question says 'You may use a diagram', it is always best to draw one. Diagrams summarize information in a very clear way. Learn to draw diagrams as part of your revision.

(c) (i) A simple idea needs a simple, clear definition. Learn it, with examples.

   (iii) The question gives you two ideas: 'honeypot sites' and 'the areas around them'. Write about each. With 4 marks available you are expected to elaborate.

   e.g. 'Areas around honeypot sites like Tarn Hows often suffer traffic congestion on the narrow roads. This can delay tourists, but it also causes problems for farmers trying to make a living in the area.'

(d) Again, this has to be learnt. The question in (ii) gives two clear hints. If you take each hint in turn and write a clear account with a named example and a short explanation, you should get full marks.

7 Ports (page 63)

(a) (i) Liverpool is the example given in this book, but others would do.

(ii) Two reasons for 4 marks clearly means that you are being asked to elaborate.

e.g. 'Liverpool lost most of the old trade with the West Indies. (1 mark) Now we import less sugar from the West Indies, because we grow sugar beet.' (2nd mark).

(b) (i) Check your answer with the map on page 61.

(ii) This means its links with other parts of the UK, where industry and population are growing, and also means links across the Channel with Europe. You should refer to the growth of trade with the EU.

(iii) Try to make reference to named roads.

(iv) Give details of ro-ro ferries, container-handling facilities and other bulk-handling systems. Ports have become more capital intensive and have cut labour.

(c) (ii) Both of these recent developments are likely to damage the cross-Channel ferry trade. However, you should try to suggest how the ferry companies might fight back (amalgamations, new and better ferries, etc.).

8 Road transport (page 67)

(a) Exams may include 'story'-type questions like this. Do not be distracted. This is still a geography exam, and you will only get marks for knowledge and understanding of geography. What is this testing?

Concentrate on the idea that private cars offer much greater flexibility than public transport does. Cars can go to more places, and are usually quicker than buses or trains, especially over short distances.

(b) This question deals with the downside of car transport. In (i) you should write about the loss of the countryside and/or the damage done to areas in towns and cities. Give an example of an area that has been affected, if you can. In (ii) you could write about accidents, atmospheric pollution, or

exhaustion of oil resources. Be as precise as possible. 'Cars cause pollution' will not gain many marks. 'Cars cause air pollution by releasing nitrous oxides which cause acid rain' will gain far more credit.

(c) On page 65 there is a section that explains how positive and negative factors combine to influence the building of roads. If you answered the first question you should have written mainly about negative factors, and if you answered the second question you should have written about positive factors. In either, you need detail of real places.

(d) To answer this question needs detailed local knowledge. Your answer could be written at different scales, e.g. describe a small-scale scheme to pedestrianize a street in a small town; or write about a city-wide plan such as construction of Sheffield's Supertram system.

Try to keep your answer in two separate sections. Describe the scheme first: where it is located and what is being done. Then give a clear explanation of the theory behind the scheme. You are not asked to comment on the success of the scheme, but there is no harm in giving your views if they are explained briefly and are supported by evidence.

9 Farming in southern Italy (page 72)

(a) (i) You must learn where to mark this boundary on the map. Check on page 68.

(ii) The 'easy catchphrase' is the best way to remember this:
• Hot dry summers (with easterly winds)
• Warm wet winters (with westerly winds).

The best candidates for the exam will learn statistics to illustrate their answers. Are you aiming to get a good mark? Have you learnt the statistics?

(iii) There is 1 mark for describing the relief. The other marks are for explaining how the relief affects soil, suitability of the land for machinery, etc.

(iv) They mainly produce food for the family who farm the land. Their main aim is not to produce cash crops for the market.

(v) The main markets are in northern Italy and further north in the EU (1 mark). Southern Italy is distant from this market and road links are still poor (2nd mark).

(b) (i) The office for the development of the southern region of Italy.

(ii) You have to choose any of the following policies listed under these headings on page 71:

Farming improvements
- Took land from the big absentee landlords and broke it up into small plots.
- Small farmers were given cheap loans to invest in farm improvements.
- Agricultural colleges were set up to introduce new methods to the area.
- Reforestation schemes and river control schemes were introduced.

Infrastructure
- Roads to link rural areas to the towns, and to link the South to the North.
- Drainage and sewerage systems, to improve health.
- Water supply, for domestic use and to improve irrigation.
- Electricity supply.

Industrial development, health care, etc.
- Increased employment opportunities.
- Raised living standards.
- Increased local market for agricultural produce.

(iii) The EU policy to develop the poor agricultural areas in southern Europe.

(iv) Its policies include:

Farming
- Improve olive and vine growing.
- Improve animal care, especially through better veterinary care.
- Improve market organizations.

Creating off-farm jobs
- Craft activities.
- Small-scale industries.
- Small hotels, campsites, etc.

Other activities
- Improve fishing by modernizing ports and buying new boats.
- Extend forestry and reduce soil erosion.
- Education and training.

(c) Describe some of the achievements and some of the problems that remain. You must also attempt to summarize whether the policies have been successful or not. The Mezzogiorno still has problems, but would they be even worse without the Cassa and the IMP?

10 The Ruhr conurbation and industrial change (page 78)

(a) (i) & (iv) You need to learn detail like this precisely, especially if you enter the Higher paper. Check locations on the maps on pages 73 and 75.

(ii) & (iii) The mines first developed where coal was near the surface and easy to mine in the south of the region, in the Ruhr valley. (Remember, that was how the region got its name.) Now the mines are in the north, where coal is deeper underground.

(b) (i) You are asked for two reasons, for 2 marks each. Each point needs to be elaborated.

e.g. 'All the shallow coal that was easy to mine has been worked out. (1 mark) The coal that is left is deeper, more expensive, and dangerous to mine, and so it is not as competitive in the market.' (2nd mark)

'The technology of transport has changed. Less coal is needed by the railways because of the growth of road transport (1 mark) and the use of other fuels.' (2nd mark)

'The steel industry was coal's main market but it has shrunk (1 mark). It has also become more efficient and uses less coal to make each tonne of steel.' (2nd mark)

(ii) Explain that the German government pays much bigger subsidies to German mines than the British government pays to its coal industry.

(c) (i) & (ii) Check the details on page 76, or from an example that you have studied in class.

(iii) Modern, light industry is often described as being 'footloose'. That means it is not tied to a location near to supplies of raw materials or energy like the old industry was. Factory owners can locate in areas that have other attractions like cheap labour, skilled labour, good road links or an attractive environment.

(d) Check your answer with the details of the projects on page 77. Make sure that you have written three distinct points, so that you gain all 3 marks.

11 Tourism in Mediterranean Spain (page 82)

(a) (i) See the answer to question (a)(ii) in Chapter 9. Note that the question here insists that you use statistics, **and** compare the climates of Spain and England. You will not gain full marks unless you do.

(ii) Natural attractions include coastal scenery and scenery inland. This includes the rocks and the vegetation. Try to give some detail on this. Many examiners are impressed by 'traditional geography' of rocks and vegetation. Also describe the sea and the beaches. Many areas are very safe, with an absence of strong currents and tides.

(b) Learn the location of the costas and one or two resorts on each. If you have visited any Spanish resorts you might find it easy to learn details about them, rather than places you have just read about.

(c) (i) Many people will answer 'well-paid jobs'. This may gain a mark, but you would be far better answering 'There is a variety of jobs, including well-paid work for trained people, such as hotel managers, but unskilled people can get jobs like chambermaids, and these are better-paid than the traditional farming and fishing jobs.

(ii) Again many people will give a simple answer by referring to 'pollution'. The topic can easily be developed to discuss the noise pollution brought by aeroplanes or by people leaving clubs in the early hours of the morning. You could also refer to loss of the natural landscape, which may destroy the attractions of the resorts.

(d) This is a 2 mark answer, so it needs some development. You could refer to growth of holidays in inland Spain, investment in new facilities, advertising in new markets in eastern Europe, etc. Whichever theme you choose needs to be illustrated with specific examples.

12 The Rhine waterway (page 86)

(a) (i) The Alps.

(ii) Switzerland, Germany, France, Netherlands. Two or three correct = 1 mark, all four correct = 2 marks.

(iii) Main, Mosel, Ruhr, Lippe, Emscher, Neckar, etc. Two correct = 1 mark.

(iv) The Rhine rift valley.

(v) Rotterdam (or Europort).

(b) (i) A river that can be travelled along by boats or barges.

(ii) It is the furthest point up the river that boats or barges can reach.

Note: These two phrases are both in the syllabus. You must learn what they mean.

(iii) They can carry more freight, with fewer workers. This saves time and money.

(c) An easy way to start answering this question is to remember that:
• raw materials are imported through Rotterdam and move south
• finished products move north and are exported from Rotterdam.
Then fill in the details with information about the industries found along the Rhine.

(d) A good choice here is Duisburg/Ruhrort. It is on the Rhine waterway, and also in the Ruhr industrial region (see Chapter 10).

13 The growth of Rotterdam Europort (page 90)

(a) (i) The New Waterway.

(ii) Eemhaven, Botlek, Europort, Maasvlakte.

(b) (i) The area of land that lies inland from the port (1 mark) which imports and/or exports goods through the port (2nd mark).

(ii) Netherlands, Germany, France, Switzerland, Belgium, Luxembourg, Poland, Austria, etc. Two or three correct = 1 mark, four correct = 2 marks.

(iii) Mittelland, Dortmund-Ems, Rhine-Rhône, Danube-Rhine.

(c) (i) It has encouraged trade between EU countries. Rotterdam is well placed to deal with this trade. Much of the growing trade between the UK and the rest of the EU goes through Rotterdam.

(ii) Goods can be carried to Rotterdam easily and quickly by lorry from Europe. People close to other ports further east send their goods to Rotterdam because it saves time, and money.

(d) (i) Packing goods in standard-sized boxes which can be moved easily on and off ships, barges, trains and lorries. This cuts handling costs, reduces breakages and saves time and money.

(ii) The workforce can be reduced because of mechanization. Ships can load and unload quickly, so they make more journeys and earn more profits. This makes Rotterdam very attractive to factory and ship owners.

(e) There are 4 marks for this question, so extended writing is needed. Check the details on page 88 of this book. Make sure you have developed your ideas. Check your answer to see how many times you have used 'linking' words or phrases like 'therefore ...', 'this leads to ...', 'because of this ...'. Each link shows that you have made a geographical connection or seen a geographical relationship. These gain high-level marks.

14 Amazonia (page 99)

(a) (i) The graph on page 96 shows the seasonal pattern. The key point that you must make is that there is very little seasonal change. Average monthly temperatures are high at all times. You should quote figures, especially if you are entered for the Higher paper. The average monthly temperature is about 27°C, with a range of only 2–3 degrees.

(Note that in a real exam you would probably be given a graph that showed temperature in a particular place. You would be asked to interpret the graph.)

(ii) Refer to the diagram showing the sun's rays concentrated close to the Equator at all seasons (see page 96). It would be a good idea to learn this diagram so that you can draw it in the exam. A good diagram earns good marks with less effort than writing a full explanation.

(b) Here the question says 'You may use a diagram ...'. The examiner really means 'You should use a diagram if you can because it is a good way of showing geographical information'. Once again, if you have learnt the diagram on page 96, you should easily get full marks. The 4 marks are allocated for:
• heating the ground
• air on the ground is heated and rises
• as air rises it cools
• causing condensation, clouds and rainfall.

(c) (i) Each definition needs a clear sentence – or a diagram. These terms should be learnt. There is 1 mark for each definition.

(ii) Whichever feature you choose, your first 2 marks will come from these points:
• heat and moisture are always available, so plants grow quickly
• plants struggle upwards, competing for sunlight
• soils are thin, because nutrients are taken up quickly by growing plants.

The 3rd mark will come for linking the rapid growth of plants to the feature you have chosen.

(d) (i) You can gain a mark for 'To open up the area for settlement and development' or 'To allow the government to control the area and stop neighbouring governments claiming Brazilian land'.

(ii) There are two main ideas here.
- Building the road has damaged the vegetation and left soil exposed to erosion.
- The road has encouraged settlers. They have cleared forest in the areas alongside the roads.

Either point could be developed in detail to gain the full 4 marks, or both points could be stated with only a little development, so that the points gain 2 marks each.

(e) You should explain that these problems affect people at different scales.

Exposed soil causes problems for local people when it is eroded, but people downstream can be affected by deposition blocking the river, causing floods.

Reduced evapotranspiration can affect people deeper in the rainforest, because it reduces the amount of water in the air, which leads to reduced rainfall.

Forest fires can get out of control and damage the local area. Smoke can blow over nearby regions, causing pollution and breathing problems. Carbon dioxide adds to the greenhouse effect, so it may affect the global climate.

To gain a high-level mark you must look at some of the problems outside the local area.

15 A The formation and features of the Ganges delta (page 107)

(a) (i) Here is a simple 1 mark answer: 'Sediment is deposited by a river.'

Here is an elaborated 2 mark answer: 'The river current slows down when it reaches the sea. It loses energy and drops sediment, building a delta in the shallow sea.'

(ii) A stream that carries some of the water from a river across a delta. (1 mark)

(iii) There are two separate points needed here. 'It is formed from fine sediment.' (1 mark) 'The sediment is renewed every year by floods.' (1 mark)

(b) (i) For a 7 mark answer you ought to plan to write about 12–15 lines.
- For the nature of cyclones you should refer to the wind and heavy rain, and to the waves that are whipped up. Try to give some detail for each point.
- Refer to the low flat land and the absence of natural barriers to the wind or waves. You may also refer to the possibility of relief rainfall, which adds river water to the floods from the sea.
- The low level of development means that barriers to stop flooding are not well developed. The area does not have good resources to cope after the cyclone, leading to short-term and long-term problems. For example: in the short term people are trapped and cannot be rescued; in the longer term disease spreads because of lack of clean water.

(ii) The answer will depend on the scheme chosen. Give precise facts and write in enough detail to gain all 3 marks available.

15 B The population of India and Bangladesh (page 113)

(a) (i) This needs a two-part answer. Each part needs elaboration to gain full marks, e.g.:
- There is a high death rate, especially amongst children, so people need many babies to be sure that one or two survive.
- There is no social security, so families need a son to support them in old age.

(ii) In some ways the answer to this is the reverse of the answer above. It needs to be explained clearly and concisely.
- If there is a high death rate, people have many babies to make sure that at least one survives. The birth rate will only fall when people are more certain their babies will survive to become adults.

(b) (i)

Stage	1	2	3	4
Death rate	high	starts to fall	still falling	low
Birth rate	high	high	starts to fall	low
Total population	low	rising at an increasing rate	still rising, but at a slower rate	high, but now stable

1 mark each time birth rate and death rate are both correct in a stage. (4 x 1)

Award 1 mark for each correct total. (4 x 1)

(ii) Death rate starts to fall because of new medical discoveries. (2 x 1)

(iii) Birth rates fall because couples see benefits of limiting family size. (2 x 1)

In (ii) and (iii) the 1st mark is for a simple correct statement. The 2nd mark is for elaboration or explanation.

15 C Calcutta (page 117)

Pushes Shortage of land. High birth rate. Not enough food. Little change of education or advancement in rural areas, etc.

Pulls Possibility of jobs in city. 'Bright lights' of city. More chance of education in city, etc.

16 Japan (page 125)

(a) There are 3 marks available. The main stages in the answers are:

Earthquakes	Volcanoes
• Japan is on a plate margin where two plates move together.	
• The denser ocean plate slides down under the continental plate causing friction between the two plates.	
• Pressure builds up until it overcomes the friction, causing a sudden jerking movement, or earthquake.	• The friction causes heat, which melts the plate. The molten lava is under pressure, which forces it to the surface.

(b) (i) Choose any two from: coal, oil, natural gas, nuclear.

(ii) Choose any two from geothermal, HEP, wave, wind.

(iii) The answer will depend on the source of energy chosen. To get full marks, give clear, detailed elaboration. Describe the conditions needed for the form of energy then show how Japan meets the requirements of that form of energy.

(c) (i) The answers are given on the map on page 121. Learn all four major industrial regions. Yes, of course the names are difficult to learn because they are in a foreign language, but you must try.

(ii) Two key ideas are:
• most raw materials are imported
• almost all of the flat land suitable for urban settlement is close to the coast.

Each key idea should be elaborated to gain full marks.

(iii) Refer to investment in research and development of new products.

(d) (i) There are many possible answers. Make sure that you know at least two, e.g.:
• The USA is another developed partner.
• South Korea is a newly industrialized partner.
• Australia is a developed partner, from which Japan imports many raw materials.
• Indonesia is a less developed partner from which Japan imports raw materials. Japan has also built factories there to exploit the cheap labour force.

(ii) There are two key ideas. Each of them should be elaborated. Giving an example is a good form of elaboration,
• To get round tariff barriers, e.g. building car assembly plants in the EU, like the Nissan plant in Tyne and Wear.
• To exploit cheap labour for mass production of electronic goods, such as assembling computers in Malaysia.

Index